941884

194
Sart   Sartre, Jean-Paul
          Life/Situations

8.95

Life/Situations

Essays Written and Spoken

Life/Situations

Essays Written and Spoken

by Jean-Paul Sartre

Translated by Paul Auster and Lydia Davis

PANTHEON BOOKS, NEW YORK

First American Edition

English translation Copyright © 1977 by Random House, Inc.

All rights reserved under International and Pan-American Copyright Conventions. Published in the United States by Pantheon Books, a division of Random House, Inc., New York, and simultaneously in Canada by Random House of Canada Limited, Toronto. Originally published in France as *Situations* X by Éditions Gallimard, Paris. Copyright © 1975 by Éditions Gallimard.

Library of Congress Cataloging in Publication Data

Sartre, Jean-Paul, 1905-
Life/Situations

Translation of *Situations*, X
 Includes index
1. Sartre, Jean-Paul, 1905-. 2. Philosophers—
France—Interviews. I. Title.
B2430.S34A5513 1977 194 76-54561
ISBN 0-394-40845-4

Manufactured in the United States of America

Contents

INTERVIEWS WITH SARTRE

Self-Portrait
at Seventy

For the past year there has been much concern over the rumors that have been circulating about the state of your health. You will be seventy years old this month. Tell us, Sartre, how are you feeling?

JEAN-PAUL SARTRE   It is difficult to say that I am feeling well, but I can't say that I'm feeling bad either. During the last two years, I've had several mishaps. My legs begin to hurt as soon as I walk more than one kilometer, so I don't usually walk any farther than that. I've also had considerable problems with my blood pressure, but recently, and quite suddenly, these problems have disappeared. I had rather serious high blood pressure, but now, after a course of treatment with medicine, the pressure is almost too low.

Worst of all, I had hemorrhages behind my left eye—the only eye that I can see out of, since I lost almost all vision in my right eye when I was three years old. Now I can still see forms vaguely, I can see light and colors, but I do not see objects or faces distinctly, and as a consequence, I can neither read nor write. More exactly, I can write—that is to say, form the words with my hands—more or less comfortably, but I

The full text of this interview with Michel Contat appeared in Le Nouvel Observateur *June 23, June 30, and July 7, 1975.*

cannot see what I am writing. And reading is absolutely out of the question. I can see the lines and the spaces between the words, but I can no longer distinguish the words themselves. Without the ability to read or write, I no longer have even the slightest possibility of being actively engaged as a writer: my occupation as a writer is completely destroyed.

However, I can still speak. That is why, if television manages to find the money, my next work will be a series of broadcasts in which I will try to talk about the seventy-five years of this century. I am working on this with Simone de Beauvoir, Pierre Victor, and Philippe Gavi, who have their own ideas and who will do the editing, which I am incapable of handling myself. I might speak to them while they take notes, for example, or we might have a discussion, after which they will put the project together. Sometimes I write, too: I make notes for speeches on subjects that should be included in these broadcasts. But only my associates can read the speeches and deliver them for me.

This is my situation at the moment. Apart from that, I am in fine shape. I sleep extremely well. This work with my comrades is going well and I am participating fully. My mind is probably just as sharp as it was ten years ago—no more, but no less—and my sensibility has remained the same. Most of the time my memory is good, except for names, which I recall only with great effort and which sometimes escape me. I can use objects when I know where they are in advance. In the street, I can get along by myself without too much difficulty.

Even so, not being able to write any more must be a considerable blow. You speak about it with serenity. . . .

In a sense, it robs me of all reason for existing: I was, and I am no longer, you might say. I should feel very defeated, but for some unknown reason I feel quite good. I am never sad, nor do I have any moments of melancholy in thinking of what I have lost.

No feelings of rebellion?

Who, or what, should I be rebelling against? Don't take this for stoicism—although, as you know, I have always had sympathy for the Stoics. No, it's just that things are the way they are and there's nothing I can do about it, so there's no reason for me to be upset. I've had some trying times, because things were more serious two years ago. I would have attacks of mild delirium. I remember walking around in Avignon, where I had gone with Simone de Beauvoir, and looking for a girl who had made an appointment to meet me somewhere on a bench. Naturally there was no appointment. . . .

Now, all I can do is make the best of what I am, become accustomed to it, evaluate the possibilities, and take advantage of them as best I can. It is the loss of vision, of course, which is most annoying, and the doctors I've consulted say it is irremediable. This is bothersome, because I feel moved by enough things to want to write—not all the time, but now and then.

You feel at loose ends?

Yes. I walk a little, the newspapers are read to me, I listen to the radio, sometimes I catch a glimpse of what is happening on television, and in fact these are the things you do when you are at loose ends. The only point to my life was writing. I would write out what I had been thinking about beforehand, but the essential moment was that of the writing itself. I still think, but because writing has become impossible for me, the real activity of thought has in some way been suppressed.

What will no longer be accessible to me is something that many young people today are scornful of: style, let us say the literary manner of presenting an idea or a reality. This necessarily calls for revisions—sometimes as many as five or six. I can no longer correct my work even once, because I cannot read what I have written. Thus what I write or what I say necessarily remains in the first version. Someone can read back to me what I have written or said, and if worst comes to worst I can change a few details, but that has nothing to do with the kind of rewriting I would do myself.

Couldn't you use a tape recorder, dictate, listen to yourself, and listen to your revisions?

I think there is an enormous difference between speaking and writing. One rereads what one writes. But one might read it slowly or quickly; in other words, you do not know how long you will have to spend deliberating over a sentence. It is possible that what is not right in the sentence will not be clear to you at the first reading: perhaps there is something inherently wrong with it, perhaps there is a poor connection between it and the preceding sentence, or the following sentence, or the paragraph as a whole, or the chapter.

All this assumes that you approach your text somewhat as if it were a magical puzzle, that you change words here and there one by one, and go back over these changes and replace one change by another, and then modify something farther along, and so on and so forth. But if I listen to a tape recorder, the listening time is determined by the speed at which the tape turns and not by my own needs. Therefore I will always be either lagging behind or running ahead of the machine.

Have you tried it?

I will try it, I will give it a sincere try, but I am certain that it will not satisfy me. Everything in my past, in my training, everything that has been most essential in my activity up to now has made me above all a man who writes, and it is too late for that to change. If I had lost my sight at the age of forty, perhaps it would have been different. Perhaps I would have learned to use other methods of expressing myself, such as a tape recorder. I know some authors do.

But I do not see how it could give me the same freedom that writing gave me.

Within my own mind, my intellectual activity remains what it was, that is to say, a guiding of reflection. On the reflexive level, therefore, I can revise what I am thinking, but this remains strictly subjective. Here again, stylistic work as I understand it necessarily assumes the act of writing.

Many young people today do not concern themselves with style. They think that what one says should be said simply and that is all. For me, style—which does not exclude simplicity, quite the opposite—is above all a way of saying three or four things in one. There is the simple sentence, with its immediate meaning, and then at the same time, below this immediate meaning, other meanings are organized. If one is not capable of giving language this plurality of meaning, then it is not worth the trouble to write.

What distinguishes literature from scientific communication, for example, is that literature is ambiguous. The artist of language arranges words in such a way that, depending on how he emphasizes them or gives weight to them, they will have one meaning, and another, and yet another, each time at different levels.

Your philosophical manuscripts are written in longhand, with almost no crossing-out or erasures, while your literary manuscripts are very much worked over, perfected. Why is there this difference?

The objectives are different. In philosophy, every sentence should have only one meaning. The work I did on *The Words*, for example, where I attempted to give multiple and superimposed meanings to each sentence, would be bad work in philosophy. If I have to explain the concepts of "for-itself" and "in-itself," that can be difficult. I can use different comparisons, different demonstrations, to make it clear, but I must deal with ideas that are self-contained. It is not on this level that the complete meaning is found, because the complete meaning can and must be multiple as far as the complete work is concerned. I do not actually mean to say that philosophy, like scientific communication, is unambiguous.

In literature, which in some way always has to do with what has been experienced [*vécu*], nothing that I say is totally expressed by what I say. The same reality can be expressed in a practically infinite number of ways. And it is the entire book that indicates the type of reading each sentence requires, and even the tone of voice this reading requires, no matter whether one is reading aloud or not.

The kind of sentence that is purely objective, like those found frequently in Stendhal, necessarily leaves out many things. Yet this sentence contains within itself all the others, and thus holds a totality of meanings that the author must have constantly in mind for them all to emerge. As a consequence, stylistic work does not consist of sculpting a sentence, but of permanently keeping in mind the totality of the scene, the chapter, and beyond that the entire book. If this totality is present, you will write a good sentence. If it is not present, the sentence will jar and seem gratuitous.

For some authors stylistic work takes longer and is more laborious than for others. But generally speaking it is always more difficult to write, say, four sentences in one, as in literature, than one in one, as in philosophy. A sentence like "I think, therefore I am," can have infinite repercussions in all directions, but as a sentence it possesses the meaning that Descartes gave it. While when Stendhal writes, "As long as he could see the clock tower of Verrières, Julien kept turning around," the sentence, by simply saying what the character does, also tells us what Julien feels, what Mme de Renal feels, and so on.

Obviously it is much more difficult to invent a sentence that counts for several sentences than to invent a sentence like "I think, therefore I am." I suppose Descartes hit upon that sentence all at once, at the moment he thought it.

And you have even reproached yourself for including in Being and Nothingness *phrases that were too literary, such as* "Man is a useless passion," *which is excessively dramatic.*

Yes, I made the mistake—and most other philosophers have made it too—of using literary phrases in a text whose language should have been strictly technical. That is, the meaning of the words should have been unequivocal. In the phrase you quote, the ambiguity of the words "passion" and "useless" have obviously falsified the meaning and caused misunderstanding. Philosophy has a technical language that one must use—changing it whenever necessary, if one is forging new ideas. It is this accumulation of technical phrases which creates the total meaning, a meaning which has more than one level. Whereas in a novel, what produces the larger meaning is the superimposing of meanings within a single phrase—from the clearest, most immediate meaning to the most profound, the most complex meaning. This work which achieves meaning through style is exactly the kind of work I can no longer do, since I cannot revise what I have written.

Is it a burdensome handicap for you that you are no longer able to read?

For the moment, I would say no. I can no longer find out on my own about recent books that might interest me. But people talk to me about them or read them to me, and I pretty much keep abreast of what is coming out. Simone de Beauvoir has read many books to me all the way through— books of every sort.

I used to be in the habit of going through the books and reviews I received, and it is a loss that I can no longer do so. It does not matter, however, in my current work on the historical broadcasts. If I have to learn about a book on sociology or history, for example, it makes no difference whether I hear it read to me by Simone de Beauvoir or read it with my own eyes. On the other hand, simply hearing a book read is not adequate if I must do more than assimilate information—if I have to criticize it, examine it to hear whether or not it is coherent, decide whether or not it is consistent with its own principles, and the like. For those purposes I would have to ask Simone de Beauvoir to read it to me several times and to stop, if not after every sentence, at least after every paragraph.

Simone de Beauvoir reads and speaks extremely fast. I let her go at her usual speed and try to adapt myself to the rhythm of her reading. Naturally it requires a certain effort. And then we exchange ideas at the end of the chapter. The problem is that the element of reflective criticism, which is constantly present when one reads a book with one's own eyes, is never clear when something is read out loud. What dominates is the simple effort to understand. The critical element remains in the background, and it is only at the moment that Simone de Beauvoir and I begin discussing our opinions that I feel myself draw out of my mind what had been hidden by the reading.

Isn't it painful for you to be dependent upon others?

Yes—although "painful" would be too strong a word, since as I said before, nothing is painful to me now. In spite of everything, this dependence is hardly unpleasant. I was in the habit of writing alone and reading alone, and I still think that real intellectual work demands solitude. I am not saying that some intellectual work—even writing books—cannot be undertaken by several people. But I do not see how two or three people can perform real intellectual work of the kind that leads both to a *written* work and to philosophical reflections. At the present time, with our current methods of thought, the unveiling of a thought before an object implies solitude.

Don't you think that this may be peculiar to you?

I have on occasion been involved in collective work—at the Ecole normale, for example, and later at Le Havre with other professors on a project for reforming university instruction. I forget what we said, and it could not have been worth much. But all my books, except for *On a raison de se révolter* and *Entretiens sur la politique,* which I did with David Rousset and Gérard Rosenthal, were written entirely by myself.

Does it bother you when I ask you about yourself?

No. Why? I believe that everyone should be able to speak of his innermost being to an interviewer. I think that what spoils relations among people is that each keeps something hidden from the other, holds something secret, not necessarily from everyone, but from the person he is speaking to at the moment.

I think transparency should always be substituted for secrecy. I can imagine the day when two men will no longer have secrets from each other, because no one will have any more secrets from anyone, because subjective life, as well as objective life, will be completely offered up, given. It is impossible to accept the fact that we yield our bodies as we do and yet keep our thoughts hidden, since for me there is no basic difference between the body and the consciousness.

Isn't it a fact that we only yield our thoughts totally to the people to whom we truly yield our bodies?

We yield our bodies to everyone, even beyond the realm of sexual relations: by looking, by touching. You yield your body to me, I yield mine to you: we each exist for the other, as body. But we do not exist in this same way as consciousness, as ideas, even though ideas are modifications of the body.

If we truly wished to exist for the other, to exist as body, as body that can continually be laid bare—even if this never actually happens—our ideas would appear to others as coming from the body. Words are formed by a tongue in the mouth. All ideas would appear in this way, even the most vague, the most fleeting, the least tangible. There would no longer be the hiddenness, the secrecy which in certain centuries was identified with the honor of men and women, and which seems very foolish to me.

What do you think is the chief obstacle to this transparency?

First of all, evil. By this I mean acts that are inspired by different principles and that can have results I disapprove of. Evil makes communication of all thoughts difficult, because I do not know to what extent the principles which the other uses to form his thoughts are the same as mine. To a certain extent, of course, these principles can be clarified, discussed, established. But it is not true that I can talk with anyone about anything. I can with you, but I cannot with my neighbor or with a passerby crossing the street. In an extreme case, he would rather fight than have a totally frank discussion with me.

Thus there is an as-for-oneself [*quant à soi*] born of distrust, ignorance, and fear, which keeps me from being confidential with another, or confidential enough. Personally, moreover, I do not express myself on all subjects with the people I meet. But I try to be as translucent as possible, because I feel that this dark region that we have within ourselves, which is at once dark for us and dark for others, can only be illuminated for ourselves in trying to illuminate it for others.

Didn't you look for this transparency first of all in writing?

Not first—at the same time. I suppose I went the furthest in writing. But there are also the daily conversations—with Simone de Beauvoir, with others, with you, since we are together today—in which I try to be as clear and as truthful as possible. I yield my subjectivity entirely, or try to. Actually I am not yielding it to you, I do not yield it to anyone, because even in me there are still things which refuse to be said. I can say them to myself, but they resist being said to another.

As with other people, there is a depth of darkness within me that does not allow itself to be expressed.

The unconscious?

Not at all. I am speaking of things that I *know*. There is always a kind of small fringe of things that are not said, that do not want to be said, but that want to be known, known by me. One can't say everything, as you know. But I think that later, after my death, and perhaps after yours, people will talk about themselves more and more, and it will bring about a great change. Moreover, I think this change is linked to a real revolution.

A man's existence must be entirely visible to his neighbor, whose own existence must be entirely visible in turn, before true social harmony can be established. This cannot be realized today, but I think that it will in the future, once there has been a change in the economic, cultural, and affective relations among men. It will begin with the eradication of material scarcity—which, as I showed in the *Critique of Dialectical Reason*, is for me the root of the antagonisms, past and present, among men.

In the future there will doubtless be other antagonisms which I cannot imagine now, which no one can imagine. But they will not be an obstacle to a form of sociality in which each person will give himself completely to someone else, who will likewise give himself completely. Such a society, of course, would have to be worldwide, for if there remained inequalities and privileges anywhere in the world, the resulting conflicts would little by little take over the whole social body.

Isn't writing born of secrecy and antagonism? In a harmonious society, perhaps there would no longer be any reason for it to exist. . . .

Writing is certainly born of secrecy. But we should not forget that it either tries to hide this secrecy and to lie (in which case it is without interest) or to give a glimpse of this secrecy, even to try and expose it by showing what the writer is in relation to others—and in this case it approaches the translucence that I want.

You said to me once, around 1971: "It is time that I finally told the truth." You added: "But I could only tell it in a work of fiction." Why is that?

At the time, I was thinking of writing a story in which I would present in an indirect manner everything that I had previously intended to say in a kind of political testament. The testament would have been the continuation of my autobiography, but I had decided not to write it. The fictional element of the story I was considering would have been minimal; I would have created a character about whom the reader would have been forced to say: "The man presented here is Sartre."

This does not mean that for the reader there would have been an overlapping of the character and the author, but that the best way of understanding the character would have been to look for what came to him from me. I wanted to write a fiction that was not a fiction. This simply represents what it means to write today. We know ourselves very little, and we are still not able to give ourselves completely to each other. The truth of writing would be for me to say: "I take up the pen, my name is Sartre, this is what I think."

Can't a truth be expressed independently of the person who expresses it?

It is no longer interesting then. It removes the individual and the person from the world we live in and goes no farther than objective truths. One can arrive at objective truths without thinking one's own truth. But if I speak both of my objectivity and of the subjectivity that lies behind the objectivity (a subjectivity that is just as much a part of the man as his objectivity), at that point it is necessary to write, "I,

Sartre." And, as such a procedure is not possible at the present time, because we do not know each other well enough, the detour of fiction allows for a more effective approach to this objective-subjective totality.

Would you say, then, that you have come closer to your own truth through Roquentin or Mathieu than in writing The Words?

Probably. Or rather, I think that *The Words* is no truer than *Nausea* or *The Roads of Freedom*. Not that the facts I report are not true, but *The Words* is a kind of novel also— a novel that I believe in, but a novel nevertheless.

When you said that the time had come for you to tell the truth at last, this statement could have been understood to mean that until now you had only lied.

No, not lied, but said what is only half true, a quarter true. . . . For example, I have not spoken of the sexual and erotic relations in my life. Moreover, I do not see any reasons for doing so, except in another society in which everyone put his cards on the table.

But are you sure that you know everything there is to know about yourself? Haven't you ever been tempted to try psychoanalysis?

Yes, but not in order to understand things about myself that I would not have understood otherwise. I wrote a first version of *The Words* in 1954, and when I returned to it in 1963 I asked a psychoanalyst friend, Pontalis, if he wanted to analyze me. I did it more out of intellectual curiosity concerning the psychoanalytic method than with the notion of understanding myself better. But he thought, quite rightly, that given our relations over the past twenty years, it would be impossible for him. It was just an idea I had, a rather vague one, and I didn't think about it any more.

Nevertheless, from reading your novels one can infer many things about the way you have experienced sexuality.

Yes, and even from my philosophical works. But that only represents a phase in my sexual life. There is not enough detail or complexity for anyone really to discover me in these books. Then, you would say, why talk about it? And I would say: because as I see it, a writer should talk about the whole world in talking about his whole self.

The function of the writer is to speak of everything—that is, the world as objectivity, and also the subjectivity which is opposed to it, which is in contradiction with it. The writer must portray this totality as he unmasks it completely. That is why he is obliged to speak of himself, and as a matter of fact, that is what he has always done, more or less well, more or less completely, but invariably.

What is the specific character of writing, then? Doesn't it seem that it would be possible to speak of this totality orally?

In principle it is possible, but in fact one never says as much in speaking as in writing. People are not accustomed to using oral language. The deepest conversations today are those between intellectuals. Not that intellectuals are necessarily closer to the truth than nonintellectuals, but at the present time they have knowledge, a mode of thought—psychoanalytic or sociological, for example—that allows them to reach a certain level of understanding of themselves and others that people who are not intellectuals do not usually reach. The dialogue proceeds in such a way that each person thinks that he has said everything and that the other person has said everything, while in fact the true problems begin at a point beyond what has been said.

So that when you spoke of the truth which finally has to be told, it was not a matter of expressing certain things that you had suppressed, but rather things that you had not understood before?

It was above all a question of putting myself in a certain position in which a kind of truth that I had not known before would necessarily appear to me. By means of a true fiction— or a fictional truth—I would take up the actions and thoughts of my life again in order to make them into a whole. All the while I would be examining their apparent contradictions and their limits—to see if it was true that those limits were really there, to make sure that I had not been forced to consider certain ideas contradictory when in fact they were not, to confirm that my actions of a given moment had been interpreted correctly. . . .

And perhaps it was also a way of allowing you to escape from your own system?

Yes, to the extent that my system could not include everything, I had to place myself outside it. And since I myself had made the system, it seemed quite possible that I would fall back into it. This would have proved that truth for me could not be conceived outside the system. But it also could have meant that the system remains valid at a certain level, even if it does not attain the deepest truth.

Truth always remains to be found, because it is infinite. Which is not to say that we do not discover certain truths. And I think that if I had been able to do what I wanted to do in this story, which was supposed to be an account of my truth, with some luck I would have discovered certain truths not only about myself, but about the period I live in. Still, I would not have been able to discover the whole truth. I would simply have let it be understood that it is attainable— even though no one is capable of attaining it today.

If you could write now, is this what you would be working on?

Yes, and in some sense this is what I have always been working on.

Yet from Simone de Beauvoir's memoirs, we know that since about the year 1957 you have worked with a feeling of extreme urgency. Simone de Beauvoir says that you were running "an exhausting race against time, against death." It seems to me that if you had such a strong sense of urgency you must have felt that only you were capable of saying something that absolutely had to be said. Is this true?

In a sense, yes. It was then that I started writing the *Critique of Dialectical Reason*, and this was what was gnawing at me, what took all my time. I worked on it ten hours a day, taking corydrane—in the end I was taking twenty pills a day. I really felt that this book had to be finished. The amphetamines increased the speed of my thinking and writing so that it was at least three times my normal rhythm, and I wanted to go fast.

This was the period in which I broke with the Communists after Budapest. The rupture was not total, but the ties were frayed. Before 1968 the Communist movement seemed to represent the entire left, and to break with the party would have been to push oneself into a kind of exile. When you were cut off from the left, you either moved to the right, as many former Socialists did, or stayed in a kind of limbo where the only thing you could do was to go as far as you could in thinking what the Communists did not want you to think.

Writing the *Critique of Dialectical Response* represented for me a way of settling my accounts with my own thought beyond the Communist Party's sphere of influence over thought. The *Critique* is a Marxist work written against the Communists. I felt that true Marxism had been completely twisted and falsified by the Communists. Right now, I no longer think exactly the same thing.

We will return to this. Wasn't the feeling of urgency also caused by the first signs that you were growing old? In 1954, in Moscow, you had your first problem with health.

It was a rather mild incident—an attack of hypertension —that I felt was a momentary inconvenience due to overwork and to this first trip to the U.S.S.R., which was unpleasant and exhausting. I did not have the impression that anything had changed. But I did have that feeling a little later, at the time de Gaulle took power. I was writing *The Condemned of Altona,* and one day during the winter of 1958, I began to feel very unsure of myself.

I remember that I was drinking a glass of whisky at Simone Berriau's. I tried to set it down on a shelf and it fell over; this was not a matter of clumsiness, but a problem with my equilibrium. Simone Berriau saw it right away and said to me: "Go see a doctor; it's very bad." Several days later, still working on *The Condemned,* I was scribbling illegibly rather than writing. I wrote sentences absolutely devoid of meaning, without any relation to the play, which frightened Simone de Beauvoir.

Were you yourself afraid?

No, but I saw that I was in bad shape. I was never afraid. I stopped working, however; for two months I don't think I did anything. And then I got back to work, but this held up *The Condemned* for a year.

It seems to me that at this period you had a very strong feeling of responsibility toward your readers, yourself, and those "commandments that are sewn into your skin" which you spoke of in The Words. *It was a question of write or die. When did you begin to let up, if you ever have let up?*

In the last few years, since I gave up the *Flaubert.* I did an enormous amount of work, using corydrane, on that book too. I spent fifteen years on it, working on and off. I would write something else, then return to Flaubert. Even so, I will never finish it. But this does not make me so unhappy, because I think I said the most important things in the first three volumes. Someone else could write the fourth on the basis of the three I have written.

Nevertheless, the unfinished Flaubert weighs on me like a kind of remorse. Well, perhaps "remorse" is too strong a word; after all, circumstances forced me to give it up. I *wanted* to finish it. And the fourth volume was both the most difficult for me and the one that interested me least: the study of the style of *Madame Bovary*. But as I say, the essential part has been done, even if the series remains incomplete.

Is this true of your work as a whole? One could almost say that one of the principal characteristics of your entire body of writing is its unfinished state. . . . Do you find that this—

That this bothers me? Not at all. Because all works remain unfinished: no man who undertakes a work of literature or philosophy ever finishes. What can I say—time never stops!

Today you no longer feel that you're pursued by time?

No, because I have decided—I say it loud and clear— that I have said everything I had to say. This decision implies that I will cut short all I might still have said, because I think that I have already written the essentials. The other things, I tell myself, are not worth the trouble; they are merely temptations one has, like beginning a novel on this or that subject and then abandoning it.

Actually, this is not completely true. If I were to put myself in the demanding situation of a man who has some years before him and is in good health, I would say that I was not finished with my writing—far from it. But I do not want to say this to myself. If I last another ten years, that would be very good; that wouldn't be bad at all.

And how do you plan to use these ten years?

On projects like the broadcasts I am preparing, which I feel should be considered as part of my work. And on a book of conversations I have begun with Simone de Beauvoir, which is the continuation of *The Words*, although it will be arranged by themes this time. Of course the book will not have as much style as *The Words* did, since I can no longer produce style.

But you are less involved in these projects.

I am less involved because I *have* to be. At seventy I can no longer hope that in the ten useful years I have left, I will produce the novel or the philosophical work of my life. Everyone knows what the years between seventy and eighty are like. . . .

What we are talking about, then, is not so much your partial blindness as old age.

I only feel my old age through my partial blindness— which is an accident, I could have others—and through the nearness of death, which is absolutely undeniable. Not that I think about it; I never think about it. But I know that it is coming.

You knew that before!

Yes, but I didn't think about it, I really didn't. You know, until I was about thirty I believed I was immortal. But now, without ever thinking of death, I know that I am very mortal. I know that I am in the last period of my life, and that certain works are therefore not possible for me. It's because of their size, not because of their difficulty, for I feel I am at just about the same level of intelligence that I was ten years ago. The important thing for me is that what had to be done was done—well or badly; it doesn't matter.

I've given it a try, in any case. And then, there are ten years left.

You remind me of Gide in Thesée: "*I have done my work, I have lived." He was seventy-five years old and he had this serenity, the satisfaction of a finished task. You say the same thing?*

Exactly.

In the same spirit?

I would have to add a few things. I do not think of my readers in the same way that Gide did. I do not think of the action of a book as he did. I do not think of the future of society as he thought of it. But to take only the individual, yes, in a sense; well, I have done what I had to do. . . .

You are happy with your life?

Very. Although I think that if I had more luck, I would have dealt with more subjects, and better.

And also if you had taken care of yourself. Because you really ruined your health when you were writing the Critique of Dialectical Reason.

What is health for? It is better to write the *Critique of Dialectical Reason*—I say this without pride—it is better to write something that is long, precise, and important in itself than to be in perfect health.

A few months ago you said to me, with a mixture of humor and melancholy: "I'm on my way down, I'm a has-been." Do you have the feeling that you are being under-rated?

Underrated? No, not in the sense that certain nineteenth-century poets and writers were underrated. But perhaps not very well known.

When you were a child, you had two ambitions: to create a work of art and to be famous. At what point did you know you had succeeded?

I always thought I would succeed, and so I never had the distinct feeling that I had succeeded. But I would say that it was after the war that I succeeded.

In other words, the burden of fame that descended on you in 1945 . . .

Very much a burden . . .

Did you enjoy it, at the same time?

Believe me I didn't, because it consisted of so many insults, and even slander, that it was irritating. But it was not discouraging—far from it, since later I found pleasure in it. But in the beginning the hatred bothered me in the worst way.

Does hatred affect you?

No, not any more. But back then I was experiencing it for the first time. I had just gone through the German occupation, which was no joke, and then I discovered that my contemporaries hated me. It was a strange sensation. And then in the end, everything worked out very well. Although my contemporaries have always hated me, what was important was that I had a good relationship with young pople. It lasted until about 1965; I mean that May 1968 occurred quite apart from me—I didn't even see it coming. And then around 1969 I grew close to young people again, or some of them, and I continued to have a young audience. Now it's different, it's beginning to change: it's time to pack my bags. . . .

Are you sorry that young intellectuals don't read you more, that they know you only through false ideas of you and your work?

I would say it's too bad for me.

For you, or for them?

To tell the truth, for them too. But I think it is just a passing stage.

Basically you would agree with the prediction Roland Barthes made recently when he said that you will be rediscovered and that this will take place soon in a completely natural way?

I hope so.

And which of your works do you hope to see the new generation take up again?

Situations, Saint Genet, the *Critique of Dialectical Reason,* and *The Devil and the Good Lord.* I suppose *Situations* is the nonphilosophical work which comes closest to philosophy, critical and political. I would very much like that to endure and for people to read it. And then *Nausea* too, since from a purely literary point of view, I think it's the best thing I have done.

After May 1968 you said to me: "If one rereads all my books, one will realize that I have not changed profoundly, and that I have always remained an anarchist."

That is very true. And it will be evident in the television broadcasts I am preparing. Still, I have changed in the sense that I was an anarchist without knowing it when I wrote *Nausea*. I did not realize that what I was writing could have an anarchist interpretation; I saw only the relation with the metaphysical idea of "nausea," the metaphysical idea of existence. Then, by way of philosophy, I discovered the anarchist in me. But when I discovered it I did not call it that, because today's anarchy no longer has anything to do with the anarchy of 1890.

Actually, you never identified yourself with the so-called anarchist movement!

Never. On the contrary, I was very far away from it. But I never allowed anyone to hold power over me, and I have always thought that anarchy—which is to say, a society without powers—must be brought about.

In short, you would be the thinker behind a new anarchy, a libertarian socialism. Is that why you do not protest very strongly when a friend swears to you that you will be the Marx of the twenty-first century?

Oh, you know, prophecies like that. . . . But why should I protest, since I hope I will still be read in a hundred years —though I am not sure of it. But I hope people will make some effort to take up what I have done and go beyond it.

Still, you must acknowledge the fact that even though you reject all power, you have exercised power yourself.

I had a false power: the power of a professor. But the real power of a professor consists, for example, of forbidding smoking in class (I did not) or of failing students (I always gave passing grades). I was transmitting knowledge; as I see it, that is not a power, or rather it depends on how you teach. Ask Bost if I thought I had power over my students, and if I truly did.*

You don't think that celebrity gave you a certain power?

I don't think so. Perhaps a policeman will ask me for my papers more politely than he asks the next person. But beyond things like that, I don't see how I have power. I don't believe I have any power other than the power of the truths I tell.

* Sartre's old friend, Jacques-Laurent Bost, author of *Le Dernier des métiers*. [Translators' note.]

When you say that, do you mean the source of your power is in the moral command you have gained through your books?

But I have no power! Tell me what power I have! I am just a citizen like any other . . .

Not all citizens could preside over the Russell Tribunal, for example . . .

How is that power? One day some people came to me and said, "A tribunal on Vietnam is going to be formed; do you want to take part in it?" I said yes. "Would you agree to be president of it?" "All right, if you think that would be best." That's how it happened. Afterwards, I was called President when I went to Sweden and then Denmark to participate in the work of the tribunal. But I had no more power than any other delegate there.

Even if the American government did not tremble before the Russell Tribunal, the tribunal still represented a force that America could not totally ignore. Your reputation for morality and that of the other members of the tribunal added weight to your accusations and could influence world opinion.

That was what we were hoping. But as far as I can tell from the contacts I've had with Americans, the Russell Tribunal did not move the government of the United States one way or the other. As for world opinion, I don't have much of an idea what it is. . . . We were hoping that the conclusions the tribunal reached would be taken up by the people, rather than simply remaining the conclusions of certain men who were following international law established by the Nuremberg Tribunal. But we can't say that it happened, that the people did respond. So, you see, I'm not clear as to what my power was in this business. . . .

Basically, you find it hard to judge how great your own fame is. . . .

I don't know anything about it. At the moment I'm no longer sure whether what I say still counts, or whether the other literary and philosophical tendencies which preoccupy the intellectual world have overshadowed me or eclipsed me completely.

It may well be that Deleuze or Foucault is more widely read these days by young French intellectuals than you are. But it is still true that they are far less famous than you, and certainly not as widely read abroad. When you wanted to meet Baader in his prison cell in Germany, the German authorities gave you permission. Why? Because you are a celebrity. A portion of the German press insulted you. Why? Because it was afraid of this meeting. . . .

As it happened, there were no other repercussions than that confounded rage on the part of the press and of some people who wrote to me. In other words, I think the visit to Baader was a failure. Public opinion in Germany was not changed. If anything, my visit turned it more vehemently against the cause I was supposed to be upholding.

In spite of the fact that at the beginning of my press conference I said that I had no opinion about the acts which Baader was accused of having committed, but was only re-acting to the conditions under which he was being held, the journalists felt I was defending Baader's political action. So I think it was a failure, which is not to say that if I had it to do over again I would not do it.

Whether you like it or not, Sartre, you are not just any-body. . . . Some people were shocked by the last sentence of The Words: "*If I relegate impossible Salvation to the prop-room, what remains? A whole man, composed of all men and as good as all of them and no better than any.*"* *Accord-*

---

* *The Words*, translated by Bernard Frechtman. George Braziller, New York, 1964.

*ing to them, only someone who is already more than just
anybody can claim to be just anybody.*

That is a colossal mistake. Stop any man in the street
and ask him what he is: he is a man, just a man and nothing
else, like everyone else.

*That man is probably submerged in total anonymity and
leading a life that horrifies him. He is simply one of a series
of numbers! Many people are obsessed by this anonymity
and would be prepared to do anything in order not to go on
being just anybody. . . .*

But being just anybody is not the same as being anonymous! It is being oneself, fully oneself, in one's own town,
or factory, or city, and having relations with others in the
same way as anyone else. . . . Why would the individual
have to be anonymous?

But you yourself, Sartre, wanted to be famous!

I don't know if I still want that. I wanted it before the
Second World War, and I certainly wanted it afterwards
too, during the few years when I was being pampered, as
you know. But now. . . .

That's just what I'm saying: now you are famous. . . .

I am, but I don't feel it. Here I am, talking to you. All
right, it's going to appear in *L'Observateur*, but really I don't
care very much. . . .

*If you wanted to be famous, it was in a certain sense in
order to exist. The other day one of my friends said: "The
new cogito is, 'They are talking about me in the newspapers,
therefore I am.'"*

Someone who wants to be famous does not want just
that; he wants *everything*. He wants to live on in the memory of men, independently of the genes that perpetuate him.

He will have readers, but because men remember him, and not the other way around. I never thought the newspapers or anything written about me would immortalize me or satisfy me. That role I assigned to my work, even before I had written the first line of it: it had to immortalize me, because it was me. And there was no one but myself who could look after me. Others can benefit by my work in various ways. But in order to know who I really am, what I am and what I am worth, a perfect psychiatrist would have to be found, and there is no such thing.

In The Words *you explained that your desire for glory was the effect of your fear of death and also of your sense of contingency, of the unjustifiable gratuitousness of your existence.*

Exactly. And once you have this sense, it doesn't change anything: one is always unjustified. And then, as you know, this idea of glory did not occur to me spontaneously—I found it in books. You're a boy like other boys and you want to be a little better than the others: that does not imply glory. Glory is an idea inherent in literature. A boy who immersed himself in literature around 1910 found in the books he read a whole literary ideology dating from the last century and forming a set of imperatives, what I called the "literature to be done." You therefore found people like Flaubert for whom literature and death, glory and immortality, were indistinguishable. So I caught it from that. And it took me quite a long time to get rid of it.

And you don't think that in a society which does not automatically legitimize its members, as the theocratic and feudal societies did, the desire for personal glory is in some sense universal?

An individual is legitimized by society if he wants to be. Actually, nothing legitimizes him, but most people don't see this. A mother is legitimized by her children, a girl by her mother, and so on. People manage it among themselves. . . .

Undoubtably. But wasn't it because you did not feel in in the least legitimized in your childhood that you wanted so much to be famous and that you actually became famous?

Yes, I think so. I think one becomes famous if one wants to, not through talent or innate disposition. But what do you conclude from all that?

I think it is hard for you to understand what you are to other people. It was Claude Roy, I believe, who said, "Sartre does not know that he is Sartre."

No, I don't. But I don't think you know, either.

I know what you are to me.

Yes, but that's just it: you are someone close to me who doesn't see me as a figure. How should I know what I am for people who do not know me? I do not produce any palpable image of myself, any image that I can perceive. There are people who, after seeing me, say "Well, he's not so intimidating." Evidently they expected me to intimidate them. There are others who tell me, "I liked your books very much." But none of that gives me objective stature. It only represents certain relations people have with me, and that's all.

But at the same time, you come across yourself constantly in the newspaper, often on television, and sometimes in books entirely devoted to you. You're well aware of the fact that you are better known to the public than most people.

Oh yes, I know that. Though at the moment I'm not sure. For the last several years I haven't been sure any more.

Are you saying that regretfully?

No, I tell you I don't care. Because I wanted to write about the world and about myself, and that's what I did. I wanted to be read, and I am. When one is widely read, celebrity is mentioned. All right, I'm famous . . . All this is the whole life I dreamed of when I was a boy, so in a certain sense I have had that life. But that represented something else, I'm not sure what. And I don't have that . . .

They say you have a taste for publicity . . .

I believe that's wrong. I have never done anything to seek out publicity.

You cause scandals.

Oh, not any more!

The proof is your recent visit to Baader.

The papers called me an old dotard. Even if it was said in order to discredit me, no one ever said it before. It's my age. You see, we always return to the same subject.

Even though in everything we have just said, age was not really the subject. When did you begin to feel you were growing old?

It's complicated, because the fact of having lost real use of my eyes, and not being able to walk more than a kilometer, are ways of aging. These are afflictions, and at the same time they are not afflictions. I can live with them, but they come from the fact that I'm at the end of the road. So as far as that goes, it's true that I am old. But on the other hand, I don't think about it very much. I see myself, I am aware of myself, as forty-five or fifty; I work like someone of that age. I don't feel old. Yet someone who is seventy years old is an old man.

Do you think it is like this for most men your age?

I don't know; I can't say. I don't like people my age. Everyone I know is much younger than I am. I get along with them best: they have the same needs, the same areas of ignorance, the same areas of knowledge. At the moment the people I see most—almost every morning—are Pierre Victor and Philippe Gavi. They are thirty. And with you, I absolutely feel as if I were with a contemporary. I know you are much younger than I, but I don't feel it.

But what bothers you about people your age?

They're old! They're annoying.

I don't find you annoying.

Yes, but I am not like old people. Old people repeat their ideas, they are obsessed by certain things, they are upset by what people are writing nowadays. . . . Oh, they're annoying! That's what old age is in most cases—punishment. And they lose the freshness they had. I find it very unpleasant to meet old people whom I knew when they were young. The oldest people I can get along with are the fellows at *Les Temps modernes*, who are fifteen or twenty years younger than I am. They're still all right. But normally my contact is with thirty-year-olds.

And are they the ones who seek this contact?

It certainly isn't me.

That is one of the surprising things about you: you never take the initiative in an encounter, do you?

Never. I am not curious about people.

Yet you once wrote: "I have a passion for understanding men."

Yes. Once I am face to face with a man, I have a passion to understand him, but I will not go out of my way to see him.

That is the attitude of a recluse.

A recluse, yes. I should point out that I am surrounded by people, but they are all women. There are several women in my life. Although in a sense Simone de Beauvoir is the only one, really there are several.

That must take up a considerable amount of time. And it took a great deal of time when all you really wanted to do was to write. You once said to me: "The only thing that I really like to do is to be at my table and write, preferably philosophy."

Yes, that is what I really loved. And people always held me back a small way from my table: I had to break things in order to return to it.

But you do not like to be alone when you are not working?

Sometimes I like to be alone very much. Before the war, on certain evenings when Castor* was not free, I liked to eat alone at the Balzar, for example. I enjoyed my solitude.

That has not happened to you very often since the end of the war. . . .

I remember three or four years ago I had an evening to spend all alone, and I was very happy about it. This was at the home of a friend who was away. That night I drank until I was dead drunk. I walked home and Puig, my secretary, who had come to see if everything was all right, followed me at a distance. Then I fell down, and he picked me up, supported me, and took me home. That's what I did with my solitude. When I tell Simone de Beauvoir that I like being alone but that people keep me from being alone, she always says: "You make me laugh."

How do you live these days?

My life has become very simple, since I cannot get around much. I rise at eight-thirty in the morning. Often I sleep at Simone de Beauvoir's house and have breakfast in a café

---

* Simone de Beauvoir. [Translators' note.]

on the way home. The one I like best, La Liberté, which is really a suitable name for me, is on the corner of the rue de la Gaité and the boulevard Edgar-Quinet, two hundred yards from where I live. I feel at home in Montparnasse. Before the war I lived in a little residential hotel for a long time—the Mistral, which still exists, in the rue Cels between the Montparnasse Cemetery and the avenue du Maine— and then in a hotel on the rue de la Gaité.

When I left Saint-Germain-des-Près after my apartment at 42 rue Bonaparte was bombed, I lived at 222 boulevard Raspail for twelve years. Now I live near the new tower. All my close friends live in Montparnasse, and I have some acquaintance with the people of the neighborhood—the waiters in the cafés, the woman who sells newspapers, a few shopkeepers.

You're something of a Montparnasse personality. . . .

Oh no. Occasionally when I am walking along, I hear someone say "Look, there's Jean-Paul Sartre." But these are certainly not people from the neighborhood; they're too used to seeing me. At La Coupole people often used to come up and ask for my autograph or question me about all sorts of things, so I stopped going there. When I'm at a café I like to be left alone. . . .

And the sort of little murmur that starts up when you arrive in a public place—doesn't that bother you?

No, I don't pay any attention to it. I know some people who are disgusted by it when they go somewhere with me. But it isn't necessarily hostile; it is usually an indifferent remark—"Look, there's so-and-so."

And do you take pleasure in signs of friendliness from people you don't know?

I have seldom received any. There are people who tell me they like me very much: I don't have to believe them.

But do you like this café life?

Yes, it's my life, I've always lived like that. It isn't exactly a café life: I have a late lunch, around two o'clock, and stay at the café until four. Once in a while I have dinner with Simone de Beauvoir in a restaurant. Sometimes she discovers one that she wants me to try; I wouldn't have enough curiosity on my own.

Do you see many people these days?

Always the same ones, but very few. Mostly women—the ones who are very close to me in my life. And then three or four men regularly: the fellows at *Les Temps modernes* once every two weeks, on Wednesdays.

Why this regularity in your habits? Each week passes in the same way as the week before, each person you see has his day, his hour, always the same. . . .

I think it comes from the fact that one needs regular habits in order to write productively. I haven't written just three novels in my life; I have written many, many pages. One cannot write a rather large book without work discipline. But having said this, I must add that I have done my writing everywhere. For example, I wrote some pages of *Being and Nothingness* on a small hilltop in the Pyrenees, when I was on a bicycle trip with Simone de Beauvoir and Bost. I was the first to arrive, and I sat on the ground under some rocks and began to write. Then the others came; they sat down next to me, and I continued to write.

Obviously I have done a lot of writing in cafés. For example, large parts of *The Reprieve* and of *Being and Nothingness* were written in La Coupole, in Les Trois Mousquetaires —avenue de Maine—and then in La Flore. But starting in 1945–1946, when I lived with my mother at 42 rue Bonaparte, and then after 1962, on the boulevard Raspail, I almost al-

ways wrote in my study. But I also wrote when I was traveling, and I have done a lot of traveling. . . .

So these habits you're talking about date from the time
when I organized my life around my working hours: from
nine-thirty or ten in the morning to one-thirty, and then from
five or six to nine o'clock. That is how I have worked all my
life. Now those hours are rather empty. But I keep them the
way they are; I have the same schedule. These days, for example, I meet my friends who are doing the broadcasts with
Simone de Beauvoir and me at my house around ten-thirty or
eleven, and we work every morning until one-thirty or two
o'clock. And then I have lunch in one of the neighborhood
brasseries, and I go back home at about four-thirty.

Usually Simone de Beauvoir is there. We talk for a
moment, and then she reads me one of the books we need for
the broadcast, or some other books, or *Le Monde* or *Liberation* or other newspapers. That takes us to eight-thirty or
nine. At that point, most of the time, we go back together
to her apartment near the Montparnasse Cemetery. I spend
the evening with her, almost always listening to music, or
occasionally she goes on reading. I go to bed every night at
about the same time: twelve-thirty.

*Music occupies a large place in your life. Not many peo-
ple know that. . . .*

Music has meant a lot to me, both as a distraction and
as part of my culture. Everyone in my family was a musician.
My grandfather played the piano and the organ, my grandmother played the piano quite well, my mother played it well
and sang too. My two uncles—particularly my uncle Georges,
whose wife was also very musical—were excellent pianists,
and you know that my cousin Albert was not bad at the organ.
. . . In short, everyone in the Schweitzer home played, and
throughout my childhood I lived in a musical atmosphere.

At the age of eight or nine I was given piano lessons.
Then I had nothing more to do with the piano until I was

twelve, at La Rochelle. In the house where I lived with my mother and stepfather there was a large drawing room which no one entered except for receptions and where a grand piano sat in state. There I relearned by myself, first working through scores of operettas and then pieces for four hands (Mendelssohn, for example), which I played with my mother. And little by little, more difficult things—Beethoven, Schumann, later Bach—with fingering that was hardly correct, but I finally managed to play more or less up to tempo, not really with precision, but generally keeping time.

I succeeded at last in quite difficult things, like Chopin or the Beethoven sonatas, except for the very late ones. These are extremely difficult, and I would play only a part of them. And I played Schumann, Mozart, and melodies from operas or operettas, which I would sing. I had a baritone voice but I never studied singing. Nor the piano, really: I never did five-finger exercises, but by practicing the same passages over and over I managed to play them in a more or less acceptable fashion. I even gave piano lessons when I was twenty-two years old, at the Ecole normale.

In the end it had become important for me to play. For example, in the afternoon at 42 rue Bonaparte, Simone de Beauvoir would come to work at my house. She would begin reading or writing before I did, and I would sit down at the piano, often for two hours. I played for my own pleasure—a new piece that I was reading through, or for the *nth* time a prelude or fugue by Bach, or a Beethoven sonata.

Have you ever played for friends?

No, no one has ever asked me to. Later I played with my adopted daughter Arlette: she would sing or play the flute and I would accompany her. We did that for several years and then—oh well, obviously I cannot play any more now. But I stopped shortly before this eye accident anyway, because my hands had lost some of their agility and I was having trouble coordinating them. So now I listen to more music than before. I can say that I have a good knowledge of music, from the Baroque period to atonality.

Almost every evening at Simone de Beauvoir's house we listen to records, all sorts of records, and sometimes during the day I listen to France-Musique. When I was writing, I never had the radio on the way some writers apparently do. But now that I work less, I enjoy listening to the France-Musique programs, which are not too bad, on the whole.

Who are your favorite composers?

I would say Beethoven, who is for me the greatest musician; then Chopin and Schumann; and in modern music the three most famous atonal composers, Schoenberg, Berg and Webern. I like all three very much, particularly Webern, and Berg too—for instance, his *Concerto to the Memory of an Angel,* and *Wozzeck,* of course. Schoenberg I like a little less, because he is too much of a professor. And another musician I enjoy is Bartok. I discovered him in America in 1945, when I was in New York. I didn't know him at all before. Bartok has been and still is one of my great loves in music.

And then I like Boulez a great deal; he's not a genius, but he has a lot of talent. As you can see, my tastes are eclectic. I am also fond of old music: Monteverdi, Gesualdo, the operas of that period. I like opera very much.

So you see, before my accidents music took up a full four hours of my day, and now it takes up even more. If I had had a choice between losing my hearing and losing my sight, certainly I would have preferred to lose my hearing; but deafness would have bothered me very much because of music.

You have never done any composing?

Yes, I even composed a sonata, which has been written out. I think Castor still has it. It must be a little like Debussy;

I don't remember very well any more. I am fond of Debussy; Ravel too.

And you have no pet aversion in music?

I don't really have any pet aversions. Schubert, perhaps; particularly the lieder. For example, there is no comparison with the lieder of Schumann. Schubert's are unpolished and melodic in a very cheap way. Take the melody of a Schumann lied and compare them!

And how about jazz? Do you still like it?

I liked it very much in the past, but I cannot feel that it is a kind of music I know very well. I can see how someone like Michelle Vian, Boris Vian's wife, knows about it, because she plays jazz herself. She is in a position to talk about it; I can't. I listened to a lot of jazz before the war—good jazz too —but really I listened to whatever happened to be at hand. And we still listen to it, Simone de Beauvoir and I: Thelonious Monk, for example, whom I admire at the moment, and Charlie Parker, Charlie Mingus. . . . I met Parker in 1949 in Paris. He told me that if he had the time, he wanted to come and study at the Paris Conservatory. If I hear jazz on the radio, most of the time I can't recognize the musicians who are playing, except perhaps for Parker and Duke Ellington. And Monk, naturally—you can recognize him by the first few chords. . . . But that's about all. Yet I believe a true knowledge of music should extend from ancient music to the most contemporary, and of course that would include jazz.

Not pop music?

Well, frankly, I don't know anything about that. I have had occasion to listen to it and I can't say I didn't like it. But I had the feeling that each musician plays without worrying too much about what the others are doing. I know someone who plays it—Patrick Vian, the son of Michelle and Boris, and I thought one of his records was very good. But I tell you—you're asking me about jazz because you play it yourself—the music that really matters to me is classical.

It is strange that I have not spoken of music in my books. I think it is because I didn't have anything much to say that people wouldn't already know. Of course there is that preface which I wrote a long time ago for the book by René Leibowitz, one of the few musicians I knew personally. But there I spoke less of music than of the problem of meaning in music, and it is certainly not one of my better essays.

And then in Nausea *there is the famous passage which could give readers the impression that you hate classical music:* "And the concert halls overflow with humiliated and insulted people. . . . They think beauty feels compassion for them. Fools."

It's true, I never felt that music is very well suited to a concert hall. You should be alone when you listen to music, on the radio or on records, or played by three or four friends. To listen surrounded by a crowd of people who are also listening is pointless. Music is made to be listened to by each person individually. If necessary, there could be concerts for symphonies—even though they too are made to be heard alone—but for chamber music, for intimate music, it's absurd.

And do you prefer intimate music?

I don't think anyone has really been able to compose symphonies; they're difficult.

Not even Beethoven?

Not even Beethoven. Though if I had to name one, I'd say the Ninth was almost a beautiful symphony.

Isn't your dislike of concerts basically a dislike of ceremonies and society events?

That may be part of it. Anyway, except for my real friends, who rarely invite me, I never go to people's houses. I have always hated dinner parties with people you don't know; you don't eat—you get eaten.

Yet there was a period when you enjoyed meeting new people?

Yes. For example, after the war I met Hemingway and Dos Passos. I met writers like Salacrou, Leiris, Queneau, Cocteau. Yes, I had the kind of relations every writer has with other writers of his time. But that didn't start until 1942 or 1943. All the writers I saw were against the Nazis and were resisting in one way or another. After the war I met American writers, Italian writers, some English writers. And then there were the ones who came to France and wanted to meet me; between 1945 and 1948 there were many people who wanted to meet me.

And why did these literary relations, which were often friendly, become strained?

Partly because of them, partly because of me. In the case of the foreign writers, there was simply the distance between our countries, and the fact that I write very few letters. I have never corresponded with writers. So we saw one another from time to time when they came to Paris. With French writers, it's different. Some I have lost touch with, not because there was the slightest disagreement, but because our occupations and preoccupations were becoming too different. You know how that can happen.

There were others with whom, in spite of our differences, I continued to have excellent relations. For example, I liked Cocteau, whom I met in 1944, a great deal and saw him often right up to the end. I had dinner with him a few days before he died. I found him very sympathetic and much less of a clown than people now make him out to have been.

He was the one who did most of the talking. He talked

about his way of looking at the world, about his ideas—
which I hardly took seriously because he was very superficial,
I think. He was a brilliant conversationalist, he was sensitive,
but he had very few ideas. Which is not to say that I don't
think he's a valuable poet.

*Actually, during this whole period you were part of what
was called the* Tout *Paris.*

I was not really part of the *Tout Paris.* It was the theater
more than anything else that led me to meet people I never
would have known otherwise. For example, I met Colette
at the house of Simone Berriau, whom I saw often because
all my plays except for *The Condemned of Altona* were put
on at her theater. She knew a great many people and enter-
tained well.

I liked Yves Mirande, who was living with her at the time;
he amused me. He was sensitive and funny. I remember one
day when I read *The Devil and the Good Lord* out loud to
Jouvet. I had only written the first act, and Jouvet had asked
permission from his confessor to direct the play. Well, Jouvet
listened to me read that first act in Simon Berriau's living
room. Mirande was sitting next to him.

Jouvet did not say a word. He was listening to me with
a frown on his forehead, with a belligerent look, and when
I finished, Mirande said after a long silence: "Your words
are caustic." That was the only comment anyone made, because just then Jouvet got up and excused himself; he was
leaving the next day for America. Poor Mirande, who was
trying to think of something complimentary to say, could
only remember that old-fashioned cliché!

This sort of thing—always in connection with the theater
—was my sole concession to *Tout Paris.* Otherwise, after my
morning's work at about one o'clock, I saw people who
wanted to talk to me, who wanted to show me a book they
had written, ask my advice about something or other. . . .

These days you still see young people who are working on your books. . . .

Yes, I still see them. The other day I talked to some students from a *lycée,* friends of Puig, who had an essay to write on *The Respectful Prostitute* and who wanted me to tell them some of my ideas about the play.

But was there a time when you found it amusing to meet famous people?

Actually, I was never the one who wanted to meet them. They wrote to me, or got in touch with me through Cau, and I said yes or no. For instance, that is how I met an actor I liked very much, Erich von Stroheim. I saw him several times. But the conversations one can have with people like that, even if sincere, always have something contrived about them. If one meets a man who *becomes* famous, that's more interesting; one sees what periods, what stages, he passes through. One can comprehend his transformation and his being. But if one sees a man who is already Mr. Chaplin or Mr. von Stroheim, one sees only what he is in the habit of allowing to filter through, and the image of his personality is there for good. It's not that he plays the part; he has been taken over by it.

And in the same way, have you been taken over by your image?

No, because I don't have as much of an image. I know that an image of me exists, but it is the image other people have of me and not my own. I don't know what my own is; I don't think about myself very much, not about myself as an individual. When I do think reflexively, the ideas I have would apply to anyone.

I became interested in myself at about the age of nineteen, and afterwards I was looking much more for generalities when I was observing myself and digging around in my conscience in order to write *Imagination*. As for *The Words*, it was a matter of understanding my childhood, understanding a former self, in order to grasp how I had become what I was at the time I was writing. But many more books would have been needed to explain where I am at the moment. When I have time, that's what I'm doing now with Simone de Beauvoir, for the autobiography.

I am trying to explain how things have changed, how certain events have affected me. I don't believe that a man's history is written in his infancy. I think there are other very important periods where things are added: adolescence, youth, and even maturity. What I see most clearly in my life is a break dividing it into two almost completely distinct periods. Being in the second period, I can hardly recognize myself anymore as I was in the first, before the war and just after it.

You see, in this conversation so far, we have for the most part been talking about my private life as if it were separate from the rest—from my ideas, the books I've published, my political beliefs, my actions, what one could call my public life. Yet we know that this distinction between private and public life does not really exist, that it is pure illusion, a hoax. That is why I can't claim to have a private life, I mean a hidden, secret life, and that is also why I am answering your questions freely. Yet in this so-called "private" life there are contradictions which stem from the present state of relations between people and which, as I said to you before, in some sense force us to be secretive and even to lie. But one's existence forms a whole which cannot be split up. Our lives inside and outside, subjective and objective, personal and political —all necessarily awake echoes in one another because they are aspects of one and the same whole, and one can only understand an individual, whoever he may be, by seeing him as a social being. Every man is political. But I did not discover that for myself until the war, and I did not truly understand it until 1945.

Before the war I thought of myself simply as an individual. I was not aware of any ties between my individual existence and the society I was living in. At the time I graduated from the Ecole normale, I had based an entire theory on that feeling. I was a "man alone," an individual who opposes society through the independence of his thinking but who owes nothing to society and whom society cannot affect, because he is free. That was the evidence on which I based everything I believed, everything I wrote, and everything I did in my life before 1939. During the whole period before the war I had no political opinions, and of course I did not vote. I was very interested in the political speeches of Nizan, who was a Communist, but I also listened to Aron and other Socialists. As for me, I felt that what I had to do was write, and I absolutely did not see writing as a social activity.

I thought the bourgeois were skunks, and I thought I could support this judgment, so I did not hesitate to address those very bourgeois in order to drag them through the mud. *Nausea* is not exclusively an attack against the bourgeoisie, but in large part it is: look at the pictures in the museum. . . . In some sense *Nausea* is the literary culmination of the "man alone" theory. I did not manage to go beyond that position, even though I already glimpsed its limitations. I condemned the bourgeois as skunks and tried to justify my existence, at the same time attempting to define for the solitary individual the conditions for an existence without illusions. To tell the truth about existence and to strip the pretenses from bourgeois lies was one and the same thing, and that was what I had to do in order to fulfill my destiny as a man, because I had been created in order to write.

As for the rest, I mean my private life, I felt that it should be filled with pleasures. I assumed that like everyone, I would have troubles descending on me without any chance of avoiding them, but on the whole mine would be a life of pleasure: women, good food, traveling, friendships. . . . Of course, I was a teacher, because I had to earn a living. But I did not hate teaching, not at all, even though I found it very unpleasant to become an adult with all the responsibilities of an adult. In about 1935 I went through a sort of depression which lasted several months and which I interpret now more or less as an identity crisis connected with this passage into adult life. But finally I managed to reduce to a minimum the social obligations that go along with being a teacher, and that worked out very well. So, as I say, that is how I saw my life: primarily to write, and along with that to have a pleasant existence.

Starting in 1936, certain political events began to make me see that that was not all. First, the Popular Front—which we had admired from afar, as Castor has said. We saw the lines of the Popular Front marching past as we stood on the sidewalk, and our friends were in those lines. We were on the outside, separate from them, and we felt it. All the same, it forced us to emerge from our absolute indifference, since we were wholeheartedly in favor of the Popular Front. But I did nothing that could have caused me to consider myself one of its supporters. Then in 1938, at the time of the Munich crisis, the social movement developed; things began to accelerate. At the time of Munich I was torn between my individual pacifism and my anti-Nazi feelings. Yet for me, at least, anti-Nazi feelings were already becoming predominant.

Nazism seemed to us like the enemy force which wanted to fight us, fight the French people. And that feeling came on top of an experience which, though I had not yet realized it, was not simply an individual experience but a social one: my impressions when I had lived in Nazi Germany for a year in 1933. I had known Germans, I had talked to them, I had seen Communists hiding from the Nazis. At the time I did not think this was important on a political level, but actually it was already affecting what I was thinking and experiencing. Nazi Germany simply put me into a rage, and there was Doumergue in France—who was a sort of good-natured fascist—and the leagues, the Croix-de-Feu, and so on. Some time after my return I adopted a position close to that of Nizan and my Communist or Socialist friends—in other words, an antifascist position, obviously without any practical consequences. . . . So you see, one can find aspects of the period before the war that point to my eventual position.

One does not have to know this in order to see that Nausea *is a leftist novel! And as for* The Childhood of a Leader, *I don't think you could have found a more radical attack on fascism at that time, apart from the Marxist perspective. Furthermore, if one compares these two books with Nizan's books of the same period, it is clear that yours are much more violent.*

It was because I had an enemy: the bourgeois reader. I was writing *against* him, at least partly, while Nizan wanted readers he could write *for*. Given his situation as a Communist writer, a writer read by more or less the same audience that was reading me—namely, an audience of people who read—this put him into a state of contradiction which I avoided. Finally, I was fairly comfortably installed in my situation as an antibourgeois and individualist writer.

What made all this fall apart was that one day in September 1939, I received a mobilization slip and had to go to a barracks in Nancy to join other men I didn't know who had been mobilized as I had been. This was what made the social aspect enter my mind. I suddenly understood that I was a social being when I saw myself torn from where I was, taken away from the people who mattered to me, and put on a train going someplace I didn't want to go, with other fellows who didn't want to go any more than I did, who were still in civilian clothes like me, and who like me were asking why they had ended up there. When I looked at these fellows, as I passed them in the barracks where I was pacing back and forth not knowing what to do, I saw something they had in common in spite of their differences, something I shared. They were no longer simply like the people I had known in my *lycée a* few months before, when I did not yet suspect that they and I were social individuals. Until then I had thought I was above everyone else. Through this mobilization I had to encounter the negation of my freedom in order to become aware of the weight of the world and my ties with all the others and their ties with me.

The war really divided my life in two. It started when I was thirty-four years old and ended when I was forty, and that really was the transition from youth to maturity. At the same time, the war revealed certain aspects of myself and of the world to me. For example, that was when I experienced the profound alienation of captivity. It was also when I had relations with people, with the enemy—the real enemy, not the adversary who lives in the same society as you or who attacks you verbally, but the enemy who can have you arrested and thrown in prison by making a brief gesture to some armed men.

At that time I was also conscious of an oppressed, battered, but still existing social order, a society that was democratic to the very degree that it was oppressed and destroyed. I knew that we were fighting to preserve its value, hoping that it would be reborn after the war. It was then, if you like, that I abandoned my prewar individualism and the idea of the pure individual and adopted the social individual and socialism. That was the turning point of my life: before and after. Before, I was led to write works like *Nausea,* where the relation to society was metaphysical. After, I was gradually led to write the *Critique of Dialectical Reason.*

Wasn't the year 1952, when you became involved with the Communists, also a decisive turning point? And the year 1968 too?

The year 1952 was not very important. I remained close to the Communists for four years, but my ideas weren't the same as theirs, and they knew it. They made use of me without becoming too involved, and they suspected that if something like Budapest happened, I would quit—which I did. Objectively 1952 might represent an important turning point, but subjectively it did not. My ideas were more or less formed; I didn't abandon them while I was involved with the Communists. And I took them up again and developed them in the *Critique of Dialectical Reason*.

As for 1968, yes, it was important for everyone, and particularly for me. The reason I had become involved with the Communists was that there was nothing further to the left before 1968 except the Trotskyists, who were really unhappy Communists. If there had been a left-wing movement after the war, I would have joined it immediately.

There was the group called Socialisme ou Barbarie. . . .

That was a coterie which consisted of about a hundred intellectuals and a few workers of whom they were very proud—they had "their" workers. . . . That was what I didn't like about them; that and their Trotskyist heritage, which they had not broken away from. And then, the only intellectual in this group that I had any contact with, since he was also at *Les Temps modernes*, was Lefort, and he didn't convince me at all. So I said what I thought about them in my "Answer to Lefort," after "The Communists and Peace," which he and Merleau-Ponty did not agree with.

Yes, and if one rereads today what you wrote at that time, one realizes that although you are again advocating libertarian socialism, there was more of it in their writings than in yours. . . .

Listen, I know their ideas played a part in the events that led up to May 1968; I know Daniel Cohn-Bendit knew them, and Pierre Victor was interested in them too. But at

the time, Socialisme ou Barbarie had nothing to do with
the will to action that arose in 1968. Today their ideas may
appear to be more correct than the ones I formulated in
1952, but they weren't then, because their position was a
false one.

*So you would not criticize "The Communists and Peace,"
even though you developed in it a Leninist theory about the
role of the party that is incompatible with your present opinions?*

I would criticize my concept of the role of the intellectual. But at that time I could not have any other idea of
it. And it was also necessary to support the Communist
Party, which the government was trying to keep from being
heard.

*You could have done that without having ideas opposed
to yourself to the point of being opposed to freedom. You
took a long detour to come back to freedom.*

The detour was not very long—three or four years.

*But why go on believing that your position during the
years 1952 to 1956 was right and the position of Socialisme
ou Barbarie wrong?*

Because I continue to think that during the years of the
cold war the Communists were right. The U.S.S.R.—in spite
of all the mistakes we know it made—was nevertheless being
persecuted. It was not yet in a position to hold its own in a
war against America, and so it wanted peace. That was why
we could go along with what the Communists were saying,
because on the whole, their objections to America were the
same as ours.

And the same as those of Socialisme ou Barbarie. . . .

But that organization was only a little nothing!

And you have never had faith in minorities?

Of course, ever since . . .

Then why not admit that these people were not wrong at the time? Your attitude reminds me of an anecdote that André Gorz just told me and that seems very significant to me where Mao's China is concerned. In about 1959, some technician members of the Chinese Communist Party warned their party against the Russians, saying that cooperation between the two countries really benefitted only the U.S.S.R. They were expelled for having "attacked the principle of the international proletariat." Then came the breach between the Soviet Union and China. The technicians asked to be readmitted into the party and the party refused, saying, in effect, "You were wrong to have understood something which Chairman Mao himself had not yet understood and could not have understood, given the historical conditions at that time. Because you have not been able to criticize your position yourselves, the party has no choice but to consider you undisciplined elements." That was the same thing as saying: "You were wrong to be right, and we were right to be wrong." That is what you are saying to Socialisme ou Barbarie.

I said nothing of the sort, for the good reason that they had not understood something which I had not yet understood either. They had their ideas, I had mine, and we did not agree on the position that should be taken where the Communists were concerned. Just because my present feelings about the Communists are the same as theirs were then does not mean that their reasons were necessarily the right ones. The facts have become what they are. What matters is how they became what they are, and the work one does for oneself and with others in order to arrive at them. Without this work, a truth may be nothing more than a true error.

Then let's say that they saved time. Someone like Cohn-Bendit, with whom you are once again essentially in agreement about political options, saved time because of them.

It's possible, but not at all certain. What you call "saving time" can make you lose it later, or vice versa. It isn't settled in advance.

What did you think was profoundly original about May 1968?

For me, the movement in May was the first large-scale social movement which temporarily brought about something akin to freedom and which then tried to conceive of what freedom in action is. And this movement produced people—including me—who decided that now they had to try to describe positively what freedom is when it is conceived as a political end. What were the people really demanding from the barricades in May 1968? Nothing, or at least nothing specific that power could have given them. In other words, they were asking for everything: freedom. They weren't asking for power and they didn't try to take it. For them, and for us today, it is the social structure itself that must be abolished, since it permits the exercise of power. This is what I would like to show in a book to be called "Power and Freedom" that I will try to write soon.

It is precisely in connection with this subject that I see a paradox in your attitude, even after 1968. Going by what you have said, one would have expected to see you associated with a group like Vive la Révolution in 1970–1971. After all, they were trying to put into practice this new libertarian spirit that had appeared on the barricades of May 1968. Instead, you backed the former Gauche Prolétarienne, which was a hyper-hierarchical group operating according to traditional Leninist ideas about the organization of the vanguard of the Communist Party.

The Maoists actually were very hierarchical, although they did not want to be. On the other hand, they were trying to join the masses not as an avant-garde but as militants expressing the will of the masses. Since they wanted both organized and spontaneous masses, they contradicted themselves. That's the way the Maoists were. As for me, two years after 1968 I was still thinking about what had happened, which I did not understand very clearly. I hadn't seen what these young people wanted, or what role could be played by old guys like myself in this business. So I went along with them, heaped them with congratulations, talked to them at the Sorbonne—but that didn't mean anything. I didn't really understand until afterwards, when I was in closer contact with the Maoists. At first, when they asked me to be the editor of *La Cause du peuple*, they only intended to make use of me. But they told me so; there was nothing Machiavellian about it, and I was aware of their purpose when I agreed. And then later our association became something completely different from the relations between a well-known intellectual and a group he supported.

Yet what strikes me about your political career is the way you have always tagged along. With the sole exception of the group Socialisme et Liberté, which was founded in 1941 mainly on your initiative, and perhaps also the R.D.R. [Rassemblement Démocratique Révolutionnaire] in 1948, you have always conceived of your political engagement as solidarity with a movement that is already in existence.

It isn't a matter of tagging along. It is because I believe that it isn't up to intellectuals to form groups. I don't mean that I think an intellectual should serve only as a supporter. No, he should be part of the group and participate in its action, firmly maintaining the principles and criticizing the action if it moves away from those principles. At the moment, that is how I conceive the role of the intellectual. But the intellectual as a man who thinks for others must disappear: thinking for others is an absurdity which condemns the very notion of the intellectual.

Yet we are in a situation where the intellectual is still necessary. Consequently, he must do his intellectual work and not "infiltrate" a factory as you preached in 1971, while you peacefully continued to write your Flaubert.

Oh, you're exaggerating. I never said that all intellectuals should infiltrate. I said they should transcend their contradictions by finding other ways of becoming engaged than signing petitions or writing articles for other intellectuals. "Infiltrating" was one of these ways. And the intellectuals who did infiltrate are none the worse for it, even if they are doing other things now. As for me, if I had gone and knocked at a factory door asking to be taken on as a semiskilled worker, it would have been a farce, if only because I was already far beyond the retirement age. What did you expect? It was not until I was around sixty-seven that I completely understood what the relation between a man and politics should be and what the true situation of a political man is —in the sense that every man is a political man. This understanding, which in a way I owe to Maoism, could not bring with it the same practical consequences for me as it could for a man who was younger and in better health.

You mean to say that if you had been forty or fifty years old, you would have yielded to the guilt-creating pressure which the Maoists exert on intellectuals and would have given up doing what you liked to do?

I wouldn't have given up anything. Nothing would have stopped me from continuing to write what I thought I could and should write and what I wanted to write. Pierre Victor asked me to write a popular novel instead of going on with the *Flaubert*: I never for a moment thought of doing that.

Yet didn't you consider writing a love story at one point?

Oh, that was much earlier! That was a time in about 1961 or 1962 when I was in Rome and did not know what to write just then. So I tried to think of a subject for a novel. Sometimes it was a love story, sometimes it was about a man wandering through the streets of Rome looking at the moon and thinking about what his place was in the history of the world. . . .

The "man alone" again?

I suppose so, but very different. . . .

Except for your intimate friends, the "family," as you call them, you see very few people these days. Do you also shut your door to the people who are writing about your work?

No, I am happy to see people who are working on me and who can use my help. Like this young critic whom you know, Michel Sicard, who is doing a study of *The Idiot of the Family.* Quite often students from British or American universities who are preparing theses on some aspect of my work have questions to ask me which are only ambiguously answered in my books. There are so many possible interpretations of the few things a writer says. So one may as well take advantage of the fact that he is still alive. . . .

Has it ever happened the other way around, that commentators have elucidated certain aspects of your work for you?

No. I have never learned anything from any of my commentators. After 1945 I thought it would happen, that one day someone would write something about me which would illuminate some of my thinking for me. I could see that when one read Zola or Hugo in 1940 or 1945, one put things into them that they had not consciously put there, and as a result one interpreted them differently. So I thought it would be the same for a living writer. But it's not true: you have to be dead for that. Or else the commentator himself has to be more advanced than the writer he is studying, has to have gone full circle, so that he is already a little further ahead than the writer. But that is very, very rare.

There is nothing really useful in the enormous mass of writing that has already been devoted to you?

That would be going too far. But I can say that in everything I have read about myself—of course I haven't read everything, hardly a tenth—I haven't learned anything.

Either I find an accurate presentation of my ideas, at best, or else I cannot see any value in the arguments against me, because they are based on a flagrant misunderstanding, in my opinion, of what I was trying to say.

In any case, there is one person who has constantly struggled with your ideas for a long time, and that's your old friend Raymond Aron.

But I know Aron's ideas too well. I know too well where he's going. As far as my work is concerned, I went beyond his point of view long ago. When he writes about me, he presents his own thinking and does not add anything where mine is concerned. I read his last book, where he argues against the *Critique of Dialectical Reason.* He poses problems and questions that he has a right to pose from his point of view but which don't concern me at all. I believe that he presents a travesty of my thinking in order to argue against it more effectively.

With more sadness than bitterness, actually, Aron says that you have never answered his arguments except with insults. . . .

I have insulted him very little in my life. I insulted him, if you want to call it that, in 1968, because his position seemed to me intolerable. That this professor, who was intelligent and educated, did not think May 1968 any more important than he did showed the limits of his intelligence and his knowledge. He did not understand what was going on.

That is not necessarily a reason for insulting him.

Yes it is. I did it on purpose. It was a way for me to take note of the fact that of his own accord he was placing himself outside the society which May 1968 was heralding. And it was a way for me to take part of the responsibility for his exclusion. Before that, he was a professor with ideas that I could not agree with, but who presented them at the Sorbonne to students who could discuss them. I accepted it all completely before 1968. But when I saw what he thought of his students, who were now protesting against the entire university system, I believed that he had never understood anything about them. It was the professor I was attacking, the professor who was hostile to his own students, and not the editorialist for *Figaro*, who can of course say anything he likes.

As a rule, you rarely get involved in discussions of ideas. . . .

I write books; there are ideas in them. All one has to do is answer them by writing other books.

But you did not answer Merleau-Ponty, or Lévi-Strauss, or Raymond Aron, even though they all wrote books arguing against yours.

No. What was the point? I said what I had to say; they presented a point of view that was different from mine. Anyone who doesn't agree with what they've written about me has only to say so. It's not for me to do it. I'm not being contemptuous: I feel anything but contempt for Lévi-Strauss— on the contrary, I think he's a very good anthropologist—but he has written pages about the *Critique of Dialectical Reason* that seem absurd to me. But it is not for me to tell him that; what would be the point?

And simple conversations about ideas?

I hate that—discussions about ideas among intellectuals. You never do yourself justice; you say terribly stupid things.

You have never discovered what you thought in the course of formulating it to someone else?

No, although I have been able to formulate ideas to Simone de Beauvoir before they were really concrete. I presented all the larger themes in *Being and Nothingness* to her before it was written. That was during the *drôle de guerre*. I have presented all my ideas to her when they were in the process of being formed.

Because she was at the same level of philosophical knowledge as you?

Not only that, but also because she was the only one at my level of knowledge of myself, of what I wanted to do. For this reason she was the perfect person to talk to, the kind one rarely has. It is my unique good fortune. There are probably many writers, both men and women, who have been loved and helped by someone very intelligent. That was the case with George Eliot, for example: her second husband helped her a great deal. What is unique between Simone de Beauvoir and me is the equality of our relationship.

In some sense you each give the other the "imprimatur"?

Exactly. That's just the right word for it. I can be pleased or displeased with the criticism that comes afterwards, in newspapers or magazines, but it doesn't really count. Since *Nausea*, it has always been that way.

Still, you have had occasion to defend yourself against Simone de Beauvoir's criticisms, haven't you?

Oh, often! In fact, we have even insulted one another. . . . But I knew that she would be the one who was right, in the end. That's not to say that I accepted all her criticisms, but I did accept most of them.

Are you just as hard on her as she is on you?

Absolutely. As hard as possible. There is no point in not criticizing very severely when you have the good fortune to love the person you are criticizing.

Then you would say the only person you really talk to is Simone de Beauvoir. But even so, something must have remained with you from your discussions as a student with Nizan or Aron. . . .

Not really. I talked a great deal with Aron and Politzer, but it wasn't useful. With Nizan, yes, a little bit. But what separated us from one another was that he became a Marxist; in other words, he adopted a way of thinking which had not been his at the time we became friends, and which contained much richer implications than he thought. All of a sudden I found myself confronting a thought that I did not understand very well, that I still knew very little about. Though I had read *Das Kapital*, I had read without understanding, that is, without being changed. And this thought became irritating —sort of devilish, grimacing, facetious—because someone else, someone I cared about, was making use of it both as a serious truth and as something he was mocking me with.

I felt that Marxism was challenging me because it was the thinking of a friend and it was cutting across our friendship. And at least until the war, Marxism remained something which bothered me, which hurt me, which showed me that I didn't know everything, far from it, and that I had to learn. And I couldn't manage to learn. At one point, in Le Havre, I read some works by Marx or on Marx. But I couldn't remember them; I couldn't see what their meaning was.

During the war, during the Ocupation, when I was part of a resistance group in which there were Communists, Marxism began to seem powerful to me. And then after the war, I filled dozens of notebooks with notes for a treatise on ethics. Unfortunately I lost those notes, which amounted to a discussion on Marxism.

Do you still maintain that existentialism is autonomous within Marxism, as you said in 1957?

Yes, completely.

So you still accept the label of "existentialist"?

The word is ridiculous. Besides, as you know, it wasn't I who chose it: they stuck it on me and I accepted it. These days I wouldn't. But no one calls me "existentialist" any more except in textbooks, where it doesn't mean anything.

As far as labels go, do you prefer "existentialist" to "Marxist"?

If a label is absolutely necessary, I would like "existentialist" better.

There is one test which existentialism has not had to pass, and that is the test of power. Today many people maintain that in establishing itself as the ideology of a power—the Soviet power—Marxism has revealed its underlying nature as a theory of power. What do you think?

I think it is true, in the sense that even though it has been distorted in the U.S.S.R., Marxism is still an element of the Soviet system. Marxism is not at all a nineteenth-century German or English philosophy which has been used to cover up for a twentieth-century dictatorship. I think that Marxism is really at the heart of the Soviet system and that it hasn't been robbed of its validity by the Soviets.

But you also think the Soviet regime is a total failure. Doesn't this weaken what you said in 1957: "Marxism is the ultimate philosophy of our time."

I think the essential aspects of Marxism are still valid:

the class struggle, surplus value, and so on. It was the element of power contained in Marxism that was taken up by the Soviets. As a philosophy of power, I think Marxism showed what it was made of in Soviet Russia. Today I feel, as I try to suggest in *On a raison de se révolter*, that another way of thinking is necessary. We must develop a way of thinking which takes Marxism into account in order to go beyond it, to reject it and take it up again, to absorb it. That is the condition for arriving at a true socialism.

I believe that along with other thinkers today, I have indicated various paths by which one might go beyond Marxism. That is the direction in which I would like to work now, but I am too old. All I hope is that my work will be taken up by others. I hope, for example, that Pierre Victor will carry out both the intellectual work and the militant activities that he wants to.

And it is Pierre Victor that you think most likely to perform such work successfully?

Yes. Of all the people I have known, he is the only one who completely satisfies me from this point of view.

What you seem to appreciate in him is his radical ambition. And that is also what you appreciated in Giacometti.

Yes, it's exactly the same thing. Nizan's ambition was not as radical. The Communist Party prevented him from going as far as he could in his radicalness. If he hadn't died, perhaps he would have become more radical, because the party betrayed him, he said.

Aren't the people you fully respect the ones who have a "thirst for the absolute," as they used to say in the nineteenth century?

Yes, certainly: the ones who want everything. That's what I wanted myself. Naturally one doesn't succeed in everything, but one must want everything.

*Are there others among your contemporaries whom you
fully respect? In 1960, for example, you proclaimed your
respect and friendship for Fidel Castro.*

Yes, but I don't know what's happened to him. He rejected us when we protested against the imprisonment of
Padilla. He was violently against us, and we were against him,
though less violently because I still felt some friendship in
my heart of hearts for the man I had known. I had liked him,
it was unusual; I had liked him very much.

And who else?

Mao. I have full respect for Mao, at least I did up to a
few years ago. I didn't understand the "cultural revolution"
very well. Not that I'm in the least opposed to it, but I
haven't managed to form a clear idea of what it means, and I
don't think it actually is very clear.

One of the last trips I would like to make would be a trip
to China. I saw it at a certain point in its history, in 1955.
And then came the "cultural revolution." I would like to see
it again now; I think I would understand it better.

*What about admiration: do you feel admiration for any-
one?*

No. I don't admire anyone, and I would not want anyone
to admire me. There is no reason for men to be admired: they
are all alike, all equal. What is important is what they do.

*Yet one day you told me that you admired Victor
Hugo. . . .*

Oh, not very much. I cannot tell you exactly what I feel
about Hugo. There are many things to criticize in him, and
other things that are really very beautiful. It is confused
and mixed up, and so I got out of it by saying that I admired
him. But the truth is that I don't admire him any more than
anyone else. No, admiration is a feeling which involves the

assumption that one is inferior to the person one admires. As you know, I believe all men are equal, so that admiration has no place among men. Esteem—that is the true feeling one man could be expected to show for another.

More than love?

No, love and esteem are two aspects of the same reality. Which does not mean that esteem is absolutely necessary to love, or love to esteem. But when both are present, one has the true attitude of one man toward another. We haven't arrived at that point. We will be there when the subjective has been completely uncovered.

But how do you explain to yourself the fact that you are inconstant in friendship and constant in your love relationships?

I am not inconstant in friendship. Let us say, if you like, that my friendships have not counted as much as my love relationships. Why do you say that I am inconstant?

I am thinking of Camus, for example.

But I was never against Camus. I was against the paper he sent to *Les Temps modernes* which called me "Monsieur le directeur" and was full of crazy ideas about Francis Jeanson's article.[1] He could have responded to Jeanson, but not the way he did: it was his article that made me angry.

And the break that followed it did not affect you?

No, not really. We had already been seeing much less of each other, and during the last few years every time we met he would blow up at me. It had not yet come to a falling-out, but it had become less pleasant. He had changed a good deal, Camus had. In the beginning he did not yet know that he was a good writer; he was a funny guy and we had good times together. His language was very racy—so was mine, for that

* *Les Temps modernes*, no. 82, August 1952.

matter—we told filthy stories one after another, and his wife and Simone de Beauvoir pretended to be shocked. For two or three years I had really good relations with him. We could not go far on the intellectual level because he grew alarmed quickly. In fact, there was a side of him that smacked of the little Algerian tough guy, very much a hooligan, very funny. He was probably the last good friend I had.

There are really a lot of people who have dropped out of your life—mostly men.

Many women have dropped out of my life, too. Sometimes because they died, sometimes for other reasons. But in general I don't see that I've been more inconstant than anyone else in my friendships. My relations with Bost, for instance, go almost as far back as my relations with Castor. I still see almost all the people we call the "family." . . . Pouillon, for example, has been a friend for thirty-five years. . . .

Yet my relations with Giacometti came to a strange end: a misunderstanding that wasn't very clear to me, but that's another story. . . . He also turned against me in some sense shortly before his death, and I believe it was a misunderstanding on his part.

Many people are amazed that you could have had someone like Jean Cau as your secretary for so long, seeing what became of him later.

What became of Jean Cau is really of no concern to me at all.

Let's get back to the subject of women. . . .

My relations with women have always been the best, because relations that are literally sexual allow for the objective and the subjective to be given together more easily. Relations with a woman—even if one is not sleeping with her, but if one has slept with her, or if one could have—are richer. First of all, there is a language which is not speech, which is the language of hands, the language of faces. I am not talking about the language of sex, properly speaking. As for language itself, it comes from the deepest place, it comes from sex, when a love relationship is involved. With a woman, the whole of what one is can be present.

What has also struck me since I have known you is that when you speak of your friends you are often caustic. . . .

Because I know what they are like! And what I am like! I could just as well be caustic about myself too.

And if you were to be caustic about yourself, what would you say?

In general, it always comes back to not having gone as far as possible in my radicalism. Naturally in the course of my life I have made lots of mistakes, large and small, for one reason or another. But at the heart of it all, every time I made a mistake it was because I was not radical enough.

Yet people who know you generally think that one of your principal qualities is your lack of narcissism. Do you agree?

I think it would be a good thing if I were not narcissistic, and I actually behave like someone who is not. But that doesn't mean that it's altogether true. I think narcissism is a certain way of regarding oneself reflexively, of loving oneself. It is a way of wanting to discover oneself as one imagines oneself to be in what one does. In short, it is a constant relationship with oneself, although this self is not exactly the active self which speaks, which dreams, which acts, but rather a character fabricated from the active self. Well, I can't say I am totally without this quality. I tend to suppress it, and there are times when I really am without it. For example, right now we are talking only about things which concern me, so I might be narcissistic. But actually I am thinking about trying to answer in the best way I can, so I am not narcissistic. At another time, however, narcissism could return. It can also arise from the way other people consider me, since a phrase from someone who is with me can predispose me to it.

But you don't believe that one condition for being happy is to love oneself?

Does one love oneself? Isn't it another feeling one has about oneself? To love someone is relatively simple and easy to understand, because the person you love is not always there, and that person is not you. Those two reasons are enough to show that the feeling you have for yourself—the self which is always there and is your own, and which is consequently both the one who loves and the one who is loved—is a feeling which does not exist. Unless, of course, you are introducing images, and at that point we are once again on the level of narcissism. I do not think that the right relation of self to self should be a relation of love. I think love is the true relation of the self to others. On the other hand, not to love oneself, to blame oneself constantly, to hate oneself, is just as obstructive to the full possession of oneself.

What is astonishing in you is your lack of guilt.

I do not have any, it's true. Of any kind. I never feel guilty, and I am not guilty.

Yet it is a feeling you have described in your work; it is even a major theme. In order to describe guilt so well, it seems to me that you must have experienced it. I think that if you have no guilt feelings today, it is perhaps more a matter of a victory than something you started out with.

From the very beginning in my family, they filled me with the feeling that I was a valuable child. Yet at the same time I had the sense of my own contingency, which somewhat undermined the idea of value, because value is a whole whirlwind that presupposes ideologies and alienations, while contingency is a plain reality. But I discovered a dodge: to attribute value to myself because I had a sense of contingency when others did not. So I became the man who talked about contingency and consequently, the man who had invested his value in searching for the sense and significance of it. All that is very clear.

And you don't think that in the way you act with money, for example, one could read signs of guilt?

I don't think so. The first thing I should say is that I did not come from a family where the relation between money and work was clearly understood as something hard, painful.

My grandfather worked a great deal, but he worked with writing, and for me it was fun to do nothing but read and write. There were books in his workroom, and he wrote, he had fun. I had seen the proofs he was correcting; it amused me. And then he talked to people; he gave them German lessons. And all that was earning him money. As you can see, the relation between work and money was not distinct.

Later, when I myself wrote, there was absolutely no relation between the money I received and the books I wrote. I did not understand it, since I believed that the value of a book was established over the course of centuries. As a consequence, the money that my books earned for me was itself a sort of contingent sign. You might say that the first relation between money and my life endured. It is a stupid relation.

There was my work, my way of living, my efforts which I enjoyed—for I have always been happy when I am writing. And my position as professor, which was somewhat tied to all that, did not annoy me. I liked what I was doing. Under those circumstances, what need was there for anyone to give me money? And yet people did.

When we spoke of guilt, I was thinking more of how you give money away.

In order to give it away, I have to have it first. I could not give any away until I was eighteen or nineteen years old, when I was at the Ecole normale and gave lessons to private pupils, and therefore received money. Then I had a little and I was able to give some of it away. But what exactly was I giving? The paper money that I received after doing work which satisfied me. I did not feel at first hand the value of the coin, its weight, its heaviness. I felt the paper bills which I gave away as I received them, for nothing.

You might have wanted to buy things, possess things.

That happened too. I did not give away everything I received; therefore I bought things for myself. But I never wanted to have my own house or apartment. Having said that, I don't think there was the slightest guilt in the way I gave money. I gave it because I could and because the people I was interested in needed it. I never gave money away in order to make up for a mistake, or because money as such was a burden to me.

One thing that struck me when I first knew you was that you often had fat bundles of bills on you. Why?

It's true; I often had more than a million* in my pocket. People have scolded me many times for carrying too much money. Simone de Beauvoir, for example, found it ridiculous, and it really is idiotic. But to tell the truth, if I do not do it any more now, it is not because I might lose it or someone might rob me, but because of my poor eyesight. I confuse the bills, and that can cause annoying situations. Even so, I like having my money on me and I find it unpleasant that I can't carry it any more. I must say this is the first time anyone has ever asked me why. . . .

I know it makes me look like a big shot to pull out a fat bundle. I remember a hotel on the Côte d'Azur where we

---

* One million old francs equals ten thousand new francs: about $2,500. [Translators' note.]

often went, Simone de Beauvoir and I. One day the substitute for the manageress complained to Simone de Beauvoir that I had brought out too much money to pay her. . . . And yet I am not a big shot. No, I think I like having a lot of money on me because it corresponds in a certain manner to the way I live with my furniture, the way I wear my everyday clothes, which are almost always the same, and the way I have my glasses, my lighter, my cigarettes with me.

It is the idea of carrying as many things with me as possible that defines my whole life—everything that represents my daily life at any given moment. The idea, therefore, of being entirely what I am at the present moment and of not depending on anyone, of not needing to ask anyone for anything, of having all my possessions at my immediate disposal. That represents a way of feeling superior to people which is obviously false, and I am well aware of it.

You also frequently give tips that are excessive.

Always.

That can embarrass the people you give them to.

There, you are exaggerating.

It won't be from you that I learn there must be some return for generosity, or else generosity is in some way humiliating.

Reciprocity is not possible, but kindness is. The waiters in the café appreciate the fact that I give them big tips, and repay me in kindness. My idea is that if a man lives off tips, I want to give him as much as I can, because I think that if the livelihood of a man is my responsibility, then he must live well.

You have earned an enormous amount of money. . . .

I've earned some money, yes.

*If one counted up all you've earned, it would be an
enormous sum. What have you done with it?*

It's hard to say. I have given some of it away to people,
and I've spent it on myself, lots of it. On books, on trips—I
spend a lot on trips. Before, when I had more money than I
do now, I always tended to carry more with me than was
necessary.

For fear of running out?

Perhaps that was part of it. When my grandmother gave
me money, she would always say: "In case you break a
window, you'll have a few cents on you." Even today I'm
not happy about it when there's not much left in my account
—as is the case at the moment. And there have been periods
when I didn't have a penny. Once my mother had to give me
twelve million francs so that I could pay my taxes. I have
always spent more money than I had. . . . I did not allow
for taxes. . . . For several years now, Gallimard has been keeping something in my account to pay the Treasury with. . . .

And what do you spend your money on?

Apart from trips, I spend very little on myself, in the end.
The restaurant once a day, but always with someone else—
that comes to ten thousand francs—cigarettes, very occasionally clothes. I am given books—I have bought a great
many, but that was long ago. I pay the cleaning woman, and
I have a relatively expensive apartment—two hundred thous-
and francs' rent per month. But all that does not actually
represent what I spend every month.

How much do you spend every month?

Including everything? There are people who are finan-
cially dependent on me: in all, they account for one and a
half million old francs per month in fixed expenses. And I
spend about 300,000 old francs on myself. So altogether it's

about 1,800,000 old francs per month. And as it turns out, Puig draws the 725,000 old francs that Gallimard gives me each month, plus, usually, a million.

And where does this million come from?

Part of it comes from the Societé des Auteurs for my works that have been performed in France or adapted for radio or television. And part comes from Gisèle Halimi, who handles my foreign contracts, for my plays or for films, interviews, and so on. All that brings in much more than my books by themselves. Last year I think I had to pay fifteen million in taxes. And then I have a liberal professor's pension which amounts to about 800,000 old francs every six months. I get the most money through Gisèle Hamini: it comes twice a year and is usually a great deal—several million. But at the moment there's nothing left, and for the first time I am wondering how I'm going to manage.

It's no longer possible to help out various groups the way you used to, as in the case of Libération?

No, I can't do that any more.

Does Simone de Beauvoir earn as much as you do?

Less, but also a good deal.

And you don't pool your resources any more?

No, there's no reason to do that. Besides, she spends less than I do.

More generally, do you think that this relation to money is significant, and that if one knew the details of it and interpreted them skillfully, one would discover a truth about you that you yourself do not suspect?

I don't think so. Because the fact is that I never dealt with money for its value as money. I never used it to buy stocks or anything durable.

Actually, you could have dealt with this fear of running out of money quite differently: by buying security, as most people do. Since you did not, was it because you felt completely sure—considering what you had become, let's say, after 1945—that you would never lack for money?

On the whole, I did think the question of money would never come up again for me. Actually, it will: if I live to be eighty, I will come to the point where I am living on no other resources than the books I wrote in earlier years.

Have you ever done any work primarily to earn money?

Yes. I can think of one job, anyway—the film script on Freud that I wrote for John Huston. I had just discovered that I had no more money—I think that was when my mother gave me the twelve million to pay taxes. I paid them, I didn't owe anything more to anyone, but I didn't have a penny left. At that point I was told that Huston wanted to see me. He came one morning and said: "I'm asking you to do a film on Freud, and I will pay you twenty-five million." I said yes and was given twenty-five million.

And if an obscure or untalented director had proposed the same thing to you, would you still have accepted?

No. There was already something comical about the project, which was that I was being asked to write about Freud, the great master of the unconscious, after I had spent my whole life saying that the unconscious does not exist. Actually, at first Huston did not want me to talk about the unconscious. And in the end it was still this question that separated us. What I really gained from my work on the film was a better knowledge of Freud, and it led me to rethink my ideas about the unconscious.

Let's change the subject. In 1967 you said, "The Pléiade series is a tomb; I don't want to be buried alive." Later you changed your mind, and Michel Rybalka and I are soon going to publish your novels in the Pléiade series. Why did you go back on your earlier decision?

Mostly because of Castor's influence, and also because other people whom I asked told me it would be a good thing. And the Pléiade has also published other living authors, so it has less of the character of a tomb. To be published in the Pléiade simply represents the passage to another kind of fame. It says: I am among the classics, whereas before this, I was a writer like other writers.

In short, it is a form of consecration?

Yes, that's the word. I am rather pleased about it. And it is true that I am eager to see this Pléiade published. I think the feeling comes from my childhood, in which fame consisted of being published in a large, carefully prepared edition that people would discuss. There must be something left of that feeling: one appears in the same collection with Machiavelli. . . . And then, as a collection with critical apparatus, I like the Pléiade very much. I have almost the whole series. For a long time Robert Gallimard has seen to it that I get the volumes as they come out, and these are the only books that I stubbornly refuse to lend. I have made great use of them, and I always read the notes, because as a rule they present contemporary knowledge of a work and therefore teach me things I don't know.

However, to appear in the Pléiade represents a sort of closing of your work.

It really is a closing: I am going to publish this last book of autobiographical interviews, and perhaps I will do the television broadcasts—though you know all the problems we're having. Then after that, what can I do? I can't write a love story! I think I will be able to scrape together another volume from this and that, by writing down certain things I am thinking about. But the major part is really done.

*This is why I find it somewhat paradoxical that you
turned us down when Rybalka and I proposed to bring out
a volume of your unpublished philosophical texts, like the
"Psyché," the "Ethics" from 1947 to 1949, and the two unpublished chapters from the* Critique of Dialectical Reason.

That never really materialized. In the "Ethics" there was
an idea that I intended to develop but never did. What I
wrote was a first part which was supposed to introduce a
main idea, and at that point I came up against a difficulty.
And most of my notebooks were lost. Otherwise there would
have been something to publish. One notebook still exists,
but I don't know where the others are.

*What I meant was that your refusal indicates a different
kind of relation to your work. On the one hand, there is what
has already been published, which is final and definitive,
since you are looking forward to seeing it appear in the Pléiade so that it will be as widely read as possible. On the
other hand, there are those unpublished texts. Now, you
have always written with one principal aim, which was to
have readers. The impression you made was in the end a matter of indifference to you. But when I told you that we
wanted to bring out your unpublished philosophical writings,
you answered by saying: "No, you can publish them when I
am dead." I have trouble understanding how these texts will
be different, from the reader's point of view, when you are
no longer alive.*

They will represent what I wanted to do at a certain
point and what I decided not to finish, and in that respect
they will be definitive. Whereas while I'm alive—unless I'm
bedridden, unless I can't do anything at all—there is still a
possibility that I might take them up again, or that I might
say in a few words what I wanted to do with them. Published
after my death, these texts will remain unfinished and obscure, since they formulate ideas which are not completely

developed. It will be up to the reader to decide where they might have led me. Once I am gone, they remain as they really were in my lifetime, and the obscurities remain, even if they were not obscurities for me. . . . Also, note that I *am* allowing you to bring out the unpublished works which are completely dead—like the writings of my youth, which you are publishing in the Pléiade. I do not even recognize myself in those; or rather, I recognize them with a sort of surprise, as if they were the texts of a stranger whom I knew long ago.

The apparent paradox I am talking about is this: on the one hand, you consider your work to be finished, and on the other hand, as long as you are alive you want to keep control of it. And so in a certain sense, you believe that this work belongs to you more than to your readers.

It is very hard to know who a work belongs to. It belongs to the author, and at the same time it belongs to the reader —these facts are difficult to reconcile. And then, the reader rarely acknowledges it to be his, while the writer believes that it is his. As for me, I think that a man's work belongs to him until his conscious death—meaning either his real death in consciousness and in body, or the death of his consciousness through madness, if it is irreversible. But as long as he is alive, the work he has written belongs to him. It especially belongs to him if it is not finished, because theoretically he might amuse himself by going on with it. As far as I'm concerned, this is true of the "Ethics" and of the *Critique of Dialectical Reason.* Especially of the "Ethics"; in the case of the *Critique* there is the additional problem of time, since I would have to go back to studying history.

But where the unpublished texts are concerned, what instructions are you giving to your heirs?

I haven't yet made a will. But I would say that the editors and the people I will appoint as guardians of my work—who won't be among my family and close friends—should do as they think best.

A large number of your manuscripts are scattered around in various places and will no doubt come to light again one day. And there are certainly quite a few letters. Several years ago, you said to us that you hoped the reader would have access to everything, as you did for the Flaubert. *Is that what you think now?*

To be frank with you, I couldn't care less. My letters are not the letters of Madame de Sévigné, so there's nothing to get excited about. I never wrote a letter thinking it would be published, I never worked for style, wrote my letters as they came to me. The ones I wrote to Castor could be published, if they can be found—you know that except for the ones she gave you for the Pléiade she lost at least two hundred in the flight from Paris during the war. Other letters which must have been quite amusing have disappeared. For example, the letters to "Toulouse"—Simone Jollivet, Dullin's friend, with whom, as you know, I was involved during my years at the Ecole normale. I wrote her piles of letters, which she kept until several years before her death, and then one day she burned everything. In them I told her things about the Ecole, and I developed some small ideas. I was Vautrin and she was Rastignac. Generally, with one exception, I have no objection to the eventual publication of my correspondence—which, I must add, has been only with women—but whether it is published or not is really the least of my worries.

You have never wanted to have disciples. Why?

Because in my opinion a disciple is someone who adopts another man's thinking without adding anything new or important, without enriching it, developing it, or advancing it. For example, I don't consider Gorz's book, *Le Traître*, to be the work of a disciple. If the book interested me—and that is why I wrote the preface—it was not because I found some of my own ideas in it, a way of trying to understand a man in his entirety. It was because I learned things from it; I was interested in what came from him, not what might have come from me. It's a very good book, which means it is new.

And Francis Jeanson?

He has written books about me, which is different. The most recent ones were less interesting; I think he himself is engrossed in something else now, and he would do better to write about that. No, I can't think of anyone at the moment who is thinking in a new way by using me as a starting point.

What about Pierre Victor—don't you consider him a disciple?

Absolutely not. He came to me not through my work but for a specific political reason: he asked me to be the editor of *La Cause du peuple* so that the newspaper could continue to appear. And when I first knew him in 1970, his thinking was quite far from mine. He came from another intellectual tradition—Althusser's Marxism-Leninism, which had formed him. He had read some of my philosophical works but he did not agree with them completely. Then I had the good fortune to work with him on an idea which was solid, which held together, and which opposed mine without rejecting it completely. That is the condition for a real relationship between two intellectuals, a relationship which allows them both to move ahead. Together we had discussions about freedom from which, I believe, something emerged.

And then, more than anything else, it seems to me that you saw in him the incarnation of the new type of intellectual, the type that unites and surpasses two modes which until now have been separate—the classical intellectual, which in some sense you represent, and the militant, the man of action.

I suppose so. Pierre represented at the same time radical theoretical activity which was autonomous—that is, independent of any party orders—and a militant politics linked to a specific mass action. Now, you will tell me (and you will be correct) that Pierre was a leader and for that very reason represented a contradiction of what I think we must achieve: complete equality among members of a group, and ultimately among members of a society. Certainly the history of my relations with the former Gauche prolétarienne is more than anything else a history of my relations with one man, Pierre, who was the leader of the party and who exercised considerable authority over the group. It was an authority which in the end he realized was harmful. This was one of the very reasons that the Gauche prolétarienne dissolved itself. We had many discussions about authority, and as is evident in *On a raison de se révolter,* Pierre gradually drew closer to my way of thinking, particularly about freedom and the rejection of hierarchies, of all hierarchies—the rejection of the very notion of a leader.

You said that both of you changed. As it happens, it was he who changed, not you. Then isn't it a father-son relationship, in which the father changes the son—when the father did not have the opportunity of forming him?

But I don't think of Pierre as my son, any more than he thinks of me as his father! It would be totally wrong to interpret our relationship that way. We have the relationship of two equals, and despite the difference in age, our association has nothing to do with father-son sentiments. I should say that I have never wanted to have a son—never. In my relations with men younger than myself I am not looking for a father-son pattern.

How does Pierre's current work—these historical broadcasts with you and the theoretical work he has undertaken —differ in any way from the work done by the classical intellectual? Doesn't the lack of any difference represent a failure that undermines the very idea of a new type of intellectual?

No, I don't think so. It simply represents one moment— a passing moment—in the formation of the new intellectual. We are in the midst of a period of demobilization, of the drawing back of revolutionary forces. Pierre doesn't know exactly where he's going, but he is exploring a direction that his experience as a militant has helped him to choose. I am sure something will come of it, but that obviously does not depend on him alone. The work he is doing is a continuation of what he has done before. Even if he now challenges a number of his former beliefs, it is not a break, nor is it a regression.

Why didn't you have Pierre appointed to the editorial board of Les Temps modernes?

The question never came up. Pierre had other things to do. And then, *Les Temps modernes* has been in existence for thirty years, and except for Simone de Beauvoir and myself, the editorial board is made up of people who are between fifty and sixty. They have experienced a half century of French history which has left its mark on them and which Pierre never knew. Among them there is an intimate relationship, a shared past, similar ways of thinking, a shared language. These are people with diverse and assertive personalities. Their ideas have been elaborated over a long period of time. Their options are clearly defined, and they are not eager to change them. But having said that, I am sure they would have welcomed Pierre with courtesy and that they would have recognized his high quality. They certainly would have shown an interest in what he had to say and would have argued with him. We did in fact turn one special issue of *Les Temps modernes* over to the Maoists, and we have published several texts with Maoist tendencies. But we also published articles—in opposition to China's foreign policy, for instance—which at the time were unacceptable to the Maoists.

You yourself are far less interested than you used to be in this magazine, even though it is your own.

Theoretically I am present at the board meetings, which take place every two weeks at Simone de Beauvoir's house. It is true that from time to time she has to force me to go; she says: "Sartre, that makes three times that you haven't come, this time you must . . ." So I go, I listen to the presentation of the articles, and I give my opinion, like the other members of the board. My views are taken into account, but no more so than those of the others. Last year I wanted them to publish a discussion by a former leader of the Gauche prolétarienne on the subject of Lenin's introduction of Taylorism into the U.S.S.R. Roughly, the author said that nothing else could have been done. We did not agree on this piece, and in the end it was not published. Yet I had recommended publication, even though I did not entirely approve of what it said. Pingaud and Pontalis—who in some sense represented the right wing of *Les Temps modernes*—quit in 1970 because they opposed the publication of an article in which Gorz said that the university should be destroyed. Later another member of the board spoke of quitting, but I managed to work things out by lavishing the necessary appeasements on him. On the whole, we understand one another well. We each catch on at once to what the others mean, and when the most important things are involved, agreement is automatic.

At the price of avoiding subjects which might create disagreements among you. For example, Les Temps modernes *did not take a stand on last year's presidential election.*

Well, we weren't all in agreement. Simone de Beauvoir, Bost, and Lanzmann wanted to vote for Mittérand. Pouillon, Gorz, and I did not want to vote at all, though our reasons for abstaining were not precisely the same. But a magazine does not have to take a stand on every political issue. During the legislative elections the year before, we took a definite position against the vote, against the *Programme commun.**

But we are not a political group with a narrowly defined program. A magazine like *Les Temps modernes*, though it is on the extreme left, of course, is primarily a magazine of reporting and analysis. Its homogeneity emerges over a longer period of time, through the pieces that we publish taken as a group, even if at first they sometimes seem incompatible. It is a deeper homogeneity which even we who are on the board cannot perceive right away, for it arises from combining our differences on a common base. I imagine the readers are distinctly aware of its identity, since we do have a public. Although we don't know much about this public except that it is very left wing, it has been renewed over the years; the magazine possesses more or less the same circulation it had in the beginning—11,000 copies.

Each of us marks his presence on the board almost entirely by the articles he proposes. Except for Pouillon and Gorz, who contribute a piece from time to time, none of us at the moment really writes for it any more. For instance, Simone de Beauvoir is mainly involved through the *sexisme ordinaire* column composed by her revolutionary feminist friends. And she reads all the articles that the others want to publish, and she proposes some herself. She directs the magazine scrupulously and firmly. However, the real work of editing, the practical work—what we call "putting out an issue"—is carried out mostly by Pouillon and Gorz in turn. The only problem we have is maintaining a balance, so that one personality does not end up imprinting his line

* The electoral alliance between the Communist and Socialist Parties. [Translators' note.]

of thinking on the magazine. We also have to keep some control over the frequent issues which are entirely put together by guest editors, while at the same time we must leave them essentially free. In general, these issues go very well.

For me *Les Temps modernes* was important after the war, then again during the war with Algeria, and again after 1968. I would say that if I have been less interested in it for some time now, it is because the magazine has its own life. There are no more major decisions to be made, unless we should decide to wind it up. But I can't see any good reason to do that. The others on the board like it, in my opinion it's a good magazine, it is read, it often prints articles which no one else is willing to publish. But neither do I see any reason to change it by bringing in younger people who would have different points of view from ours. One might as well start a new magazine.

Turning to politics: For a year now you have personally taken a number of stands on international issues. On national issues, however, you have taken none. Don't you think that if the left had won the presidential elections, you would now be a much more virulent opponent of those in power?

That's very hard to say. If Mittérand had won the presidential elections, he would be at knife point with the Communists now. And the leftists would probably be stronger. What is certain is that I would have been opposed to the Socialist Party and that I would have been involved with extreme leftist groups which would necessarily have been just as opposed to the Communists as to the Socialists. But it is impossible to know how strong the social movements unleashed by the victory of the left would have been. You can't ask me to take a stand on mere possibilities. As far as the problem of French politics goes, I don't see a lot that I can do. It's so rotten, what's happening in France now! And there's no hope in the immediate future; no party offers any hope at all. . . .

In general, your political statements are optimistic, even though in private you are very pessimistic.

Yes, I am. And my statements are never very optimistic, because in each social event that is important to us, that touches us, I see the contradictions—either manifest or hardly noticeable yet. I see the mistakes, the risks, everything that can prevent a situation from going in the direction of freedom. And there I am pessimistic because each time, the risks are in fact enormous. Look at Portugal, where the kind of socialism we want has a small chance now which it didn't have at all before April 25, and yet runs the greatest risk of being postponed again for a very long time. Looking at everything generally, I say to myself: Either man is finished (and in that case not only is he finished, but he has never existed—he will have been no more than a species, like the ant) or else he will adapt by bringing about some form of libertarian socialism. When I think about individual social acts, I tend to think man is finished. But if I consider all the conditions necessary for man to exist at all, I tell myself that the only thing to do is to point out, emphasize, and support with all one's strength whatever aspects of a particular political and social situation can produce a society of free men. If one does not do that, one is in effect agreeing that man is a piece of shit.

That is what Gramsci said: "We must fight with pessimism of the mind and optimism of the will."

That is not exactly how I would formulate it. It's true that we have to fight. But it has nothing to do with voluntarism. If I were convinced that any fight for freedom was necessarily doomed to failure, there would be no sense in fighting. No, if I am not completely pessimistic it is primarily because I sense in myself certain needs which are not only mine but the needs of every man. To express it another way, it is the experienced certainty of my own freedom, to the extent that it is everyone's freedom, which gives me at the same time the need for a free life and the certainty that this need is felt in a more or less clear, more or less conscious way by everyone.

The coming revolution will be very different from the previous ones. It will last much longer and will be much harsher, much more profound. I am not thinking only of France; today I identify myself with the revolutionary battles being fought throughout the world. That is why the situation in France, all choked up as it is now, does not drive me to greater pessimism. I can only say that at least fifty years of struggle will be necessary for the partial victory of the people's power over bourgeois power. There will be advances and retreats, limited successes and reversible defeats, in order finally to bring into existence a new society in which all the powers have been done away with because each individual has full possession of himself. Revolution is not a single moment in which one power overthrows another; it is a long movement in which power is dismantled. Nothing can guarantee success for us, nor can anything rationally convince us that failure is inevitable. But the alternatives really are socialism or barbarism.

In the end, like Pascal, you are making a wager.

Yes, with the difference that I am wagering on man, not on God. But it is true that either man crumbles—and then all one could say is that during the twenty thousand years in which there have been men, a few of them tried to create man and failed—or else this revolution succeeds and creates man by bringing about freedom. Nothing is less sure. In the same way, socialism is not a certainty, it is a value: it is freedom choosing itself as the goal.

Which therefore presupposes a faith?

Yes, to the extent that it is impossible to find a rational basis for revolutionary optimism, since what *is* is the present reality. And how can we lay the foundations for the future reality? Nothing allows me to do it. I am sure of one thing —that we must make a radical politics. But I am not sure that it will succeed, and there faith enters in. I can understand my refusals, I can demonstrate the reasons for refusing this society, I can show that it is immoral—that it is made not for people but for profit and that therefore it must be radically changed. All this is possible and does not imply faith, but action. All I can do as an intellectual is try to win over as many people as I can—that is, the masses— to radical action for changing society. That is what I have tried to do, and I cannot say either that I have succeeded or that I have failed, since the future is undecided.

You have lived through seventy years of this century's history, you have gone through two world wars, you have witnessed enormous social changes, you have seen hopes dashed and other hopes that were not foreseeable come to life. Would you say that we have better prospects than at the beginning of the century, or that we are in a situation where the risk of a definitive failure of the human adventure is as great as before?

I would say that we are more advanced, as we begin to move toward the decisive moment of history—that is, toward revolution—but also that the risks are the same. In other words, I don't see any reason to be more optimistic than we were fifty or sixty years ago. But on the other hand, I think that many dangers were avoided, and that there has been some progress, even so. If you had known the period 1914 to 1918, when I began to live, you would be able to take stock of the differences and see that they are encouraging.

In spite of the millions of deaths in the last world war, in spite of Hitler's camps, in spite of the atomic bomb, in spite of the Gulag?

Of course, yes. Don't think that the pharaohs wouldn't have wanted to kill fifty million of their enemies! They didn't do it because they couldn't. The fact that it is possible today should almost contribute to our optimism: it is an indication of progress on a certain level.

Which doesn't change the fact that the victims were individuals whose loss is irreparable. . . .

Of course; I agree. From the point of view of the individuals, the harm done to them will never have any justification. I am only saying that the enormous number of victims in this century is also a function of the growth in world population, and that there is no reason to despair because of it.

Have you always been sincere in politics?

Insofar as possible. There were situations in which, politics being what it is, I undoubtedly supported ideas I was not very sure of. But I don't think I ever deliberately affirmed the opposite of what I believed.

Even where the U.S.S.R. was concerned?

Oh, yes, I did actually lie about that after my first visit to the U.S.S.R. in 1954. Well, "lie" is a strong word: I wrote an article—which Cau finished, as a matter of fact, because I was ill, I had just been in the hospital in Moscow—saying nice things about the U.S.S.R. which I did not believe. I did that partly because I think that when you have just been invited somewhere by people, you can't dump on them as soon as you get home, and partly because I wasn't very sure where I stood in relation to the U.S.S.R. and my own ideas.

But when you first went to the U.S.S.R., did you know of the existence of the camps?

Yes, I knew about them; I had denounced them four years earlier, along with Merleau-Ponty. Actually it was a joke among the writers who received me—they would say, "Be sure not to go see the camps without us!" But I didn't know they still existed after the death of Stalin, and certainly not that the Gulag was involved! No one in the West knew it for certain at that time. . . .

So aren't you afraid of learning some day that there is a Gulag in China?

But we are already somewhat aware of it; you read Jean Pasqualini's book on the Chinese prison camps! When I was in China in 1955, I was shown prisons, but they had nothing to do with what Pasqualini describes, which I have no doubt is true. But I think there are many fewer camps in China than in the U.S.S.R., even if they are undoubtedly terrible. . . .

And don't you think we might be in for some nasty surprises?

Oh, yes, I think so. That's why we shouldn't put our faith in the Chinese revolution, any more than in any revolution today. But once again, that does not stop me from being optimistic.

One of the only political problems about which you have gone against the whole world in impenetrable intransigence is the Arab-Israeli conflict. And because you have done so, you have isolated yourself to a certain extent from your comrades in the struggle. Yet I think there are many people who are grateful to you for that independence.

I don't believe anyone is grateful to me. I think it is more the reverse: each of the two sides would like me to disassociate myself from the other. But I have friends on both sides and I recognize the rights of each. I know my position is purely a moral one, but this is precisely one of those cases which prove that one must reject political realism because it leads to war. I would say the Arab-Israeli conflict, with the emotional implications it had for me, played a part in making me abandon the political realism I went along with to a certain extent before 1968. And here, in fact, I did not agree with the Maoists.

Speaking of the influence of your ideas, the other day I had a strange experience. I was at the top of the Montparnasse tower watching a demonstration of lycée students go by. A woman of about thirty-five, an employee in the tower, happened to be next to me. We started talking about the demonstration. She was against it, because she disapproved of all revolts. And she disapproved of all revolts, she said, because she believed she herself was totally responsible for her fate. She didn't particularly like her life, but she believed that at each stage on the way to where she was today, she had always had a choice. For instance, she freely chose to marry at the age of seventeen instead of continuing her studies. "And everyone is as free as I am," she said, "and therefore responsible for his situation." What struck me is that she was using almost word for word a number of the best-known of our formulations. What would you have said to this woman, who had perhaps read you in school and who perhaps owed to you the ideas that justified her resignation?

Well, I would have talked to her about alienation. I would have told her that we are free, but that we have to free ourselves, and so freedom must revolt against forms of alienation. Isn't that what you would have said?

Yes, of course, that is roughly what I said to her. But she stuck to her opinion.

Well, as far as that goes, it is her business. And how did it end?

The way conversations like that always end; we went our separate ways. You know very well that in order to change someone, you have to love them very much. But I wanted to

*ask you one thing: haven't you sometimes had the feeling
that the most widely known part of your thinking—the notions of freedom and individual responsibility—is precisely
the part that is most likely to become an obstacle to true
political awareness?*

Possibly. But I think this kind of misunderstanding always happens when someone's work becomes public. The
most vivid and profound part of a thought can bring the most
good and also, if it is understood in the wrong way, the most
harm. I think that a theory of freedom which does not explain what the forms of alienation are—to what extent freedom can be manipulated, distorted, turned against itself—
can cruelly deceive someone who does not understand all it
implies and who thinks that freedom is everywhere. But I
don't think a person who reads what I have written carefully
can make a mistake like that.

In my broadcasts I will explain what I mean about this
on a political level; it will be one of the larger themes of the
three concluding talks. But I will explain it on the basis of
precise, concrete cases. It will not be philosophy, or at least
it will not be expressed philosophically.

And do you think you will convince people?

I have no idea. I will try.

In his last article in Les Temps modernes, *François
Georges writes: "If my ideas have failed to convince every-
one, it is no doubt because they weren't completely true."
Would you say something like that?*

It's well put, and it is what everyone thinks at some point.
This does not prove that it's true; there are some ideas that
take longer to convince people. Everyone has discouraging
moments. At times I think I could actually have said something like that. But to do so is both to honor "everyone"
too much—since it is the truth of the ideas that is in question

and not everyone—and to assert that true ideas triumph right away—which is equally false. What if Socrates had said something like that as he died? It would have been laughable! His thought affected the whole world, but long afterwards.

And how about you? Do you have the feeling that your thought has had an effect?

I hope it will. I think one has very little evidence about the importance of one's ideas during one's own lifetime, and it's good that way.

Letters from readers, for example, don't tell you anything?

Each is a letter from *one* reader: what does he represent? Besides, people write me less often now. At a certain time I did receive a lot of letters, but now hardly any come. And the letters I receive interest me less: people saying they like me very much does not have a great effect on me, it doesn't mean much. I have had correspondences with people I didn't know, who would write to me and whom I would answer. And one day the correspondence would end suddenly, either because they were dissatisfied with one of my answers or because they suddenly had other things to do. All that gave me fewer illusions about the letters I receive which seem sincere. And then I receive quite a few from crazy people. I don't know if Gide's correspondence, for example, had as large a proportion of crackpots. In any case, since I started publishing I have always had several of them trailing after me. I don't know if it's because of what I write or if all writers excite the demands or confidences of cranks. After *Nausea*, many people said that I was crazy and that I was telling the story of a crazy person: this could have induced psychotics to get in touch with me. After *Saint Genet*, I received many letters from homosexuals, simply because I had talked about a homosexual and they felt isolated. But as I say, the letters I still receive now and then hardly interest me any more.

*And do you have the feeling that this is what old age is—
indifference?*

I did not say I was indifferent!

What still has real interest for you?

Music, as I told you. Philosophy and politics.

But do they excite you?

No, there is not much that excites me any more. I put
myself a little above . . .

Is there anything you would like to add?

In one sense, everything, I suppose; and in another sense
nothing. Everything, because in connection with what we
have said, there is everything else, and it should all be ex-
plored with care. But this cannot be done in an interview.
That is what I feel every time I give an interview. In a way
they are frustrating, because there are so many things to say.
The interview brings them to life, along with their opposites,
at the very moment that one answers. But having said this,
I think that our conversation has given a portrait of what I
am at the age of seventy.

*You will not conclude, as Simone de Beauvoir did, that
you have been "had by life"?*

Oh no, I wouldn't say that. Besides, she herself, you know,
says rightly that she did not mean that she had been had by
life, but that she felt cheated in the circumstances in which
she wrote that book,* since it came after the Algerian war,
and so on. But I wouldn't say that; I have not been had by
anything, I have not been disappointed by anything. I have
known people, good and bad—moreover, the bad are never
bad except in relation to certain goals. I have written, I have
lived, I have nothing to regret.

* *La Force des choses*, Gallimard, 1963.

In short, so far life has been good to you?

On the whole, yes. I don't see what I could reproach it with. It has given me what I wanted and at the same time it has shown that this wasn't much. But what can you do?

(The interview ends in wild laughter brought on by the last statement.)

SARTRE   The laughter must be kept. You should put: "Accompanied by laughter."

Simone de Beauvoir Interviews Sartre

SIMONE DE BEAUVOIR *Well, Sartre, I would like to ask you some questions about women. You have never actually expressed any opinion about this issue, and my first question, in fact, concerns just that. Why is it that you have talked about all the other oppressed groups—the workers, the blacks (in* Black Orpheus*), the Jews (in* Anti-Semite and Jew*)—and yet have never talked about women? How do you explain that?*

JEAN-PAUL SARTRE   I think it dates back to my childhood, when I was more or less surrounded by women. My grandmother and my mother took care of me, and I was also surrounded by little girls. So that girls and women in some way formed my natural environment, and I have always believed that there was some sort of woman inside me.

The fact that you were surrounded by women should not necessarily have prevented you from recognizing the importance of the fact that they were oppressed.

I sensed that my grandmother was oppressed by my grandfather, but I did not realize it consciously. And as a widow

Interview published in L'Arc, *no. 61, 1975.*

my mother was oppressed by her parents, but as much by her mother as by her father.

But you're grown up now! Why have you ignored the fact that women are the victims of oppression?

I was not aware of the extent of it. I only saw particular cases. Of course, I saw a great many of them. But each time, I thought it was the individual fault of the man to be domineering and a characteristic of that woman to be particularly submissive.

Couldn't one say that many men—and even many women, because for a long time I was the same way—have a sort of blind spot where the situation of women is involved? We accept the relationship between men and women as so basic that it seems natural, and in the end we are no longer even aware of it.

In some sense I am reminded of what went on in the democracy of ancient Greece, where people who professed to believe in equality did not see that slavery existed. It seems to me that centuries from now, people will look at the way women are treated in our society with as much amazement as, for example, we regard the existence of slavery in the democracy of Athens.

I think you're right. When I was young I believed that men were superior, though that did not preclude a certain degree of equality between men and women. It seemed to me that in society, women were treated as the equals of men. In some cases a man—my stepfather, for example—might be haughty, proud, and domineering in his relations with his wife, but to me this was simply a personal characteristic.

Yet you yourself have just said that in your relations with women—and there have been many of them—you considered them as being both equal and not equal. Do you mean what you once told me, that considering their oppression, they are the equals of men, even if they are not?

What I mean is that since it is more difficult for a woman to acquire as much culture, knowledge, and freedom as a man, a woman can seem equal to you, even if she does not have as much culture, freedom, and so on?

That's part of it. I felt that she had a certain way of being, and certain kinds of feelings, that I recognized in myself. Because of that, I felt I could have much better conversations with women than with men.

With men, the conversation always degenerates into discussions of professional matters. You end up talking about either current economic relations or the Greek aorist, depending on whether you are a shopkeeper or a professor. It is rare that you can sit down with a man on a café terrace, for example, and talk about the weather, or the people going by, or the way the street looks. These are things which I have always talked about with women and which gave me the feeling they were my equals, although of course, I was the one who led the conversation. I led it because I had decided to lead it.

But there is an element of macho *in the fact that it was you who led the conversation and that it was natural for you to do it. Also, I must say that when one looks back over your work as a whole, one finds traces of* macho, *even of phallocracy.*

You're exaggerating slightly. However, I admit that it's true.

But didn't you sense a great deal of macho *in yourself?*

In a way, yes, since I was the one who decided what kind of relationship there would be, provided the woman was willing, of course. But then I was the one who made the first advances. And I did not assume that my *macho* arose from the fact that I was male. I took it to be a characteristic trait of mine.

That's odd, since you were the first to say that psychology, interiority, is never anything but the interiorizing of a situation.

Yes. My situation in relation to women was that of most men of our time. I took it to be individual superiority. But I must confess that I believed I was far superior to my age group in my own sex—in other words, superior to many men.

So that the idea of superiority did not seem to apply only to your relations with women, since you felt it with everyone?

You might say that. Yet there was something special about it, because it was accompanied by emotion. A study should be made of superiority as it is perceived through emotion. What does it mean to love someone while feeling superior to her, and how much of a contradiction is there in this?

What I think is most interesting here is that while you were willing to say that you were "anybody," you did not feel that your macho *was "anybody's" macho.*

But rather the *macho* of one particular individual. You shouldn't think that I considered myself to be "anybody" all my life. I was forty when I wrote that, and I still believe it.

Returning to the idea of macho, *we really should give the other side of the story as well. After all, it was you who strongly encouraged me to write* The Second Sex, *and when the book was finished, you accepted all its arguments, whereas people like Camus, for example, almost threw the book in my face. And it was then that I discovered the male chauvinism of a number of men whom I had believed to be truly democratic in their attitudes toward sex as well as toward society in general.*

Yes, but first I should say that in our own relationship I have always considered you to be my equal.

I have to say that you have never oppressed me, and that you have never acted superior to me. To offset the idea of your macho, *it is important to realize that we have never had an inferiority-superiority relationship, as men and women so often do.*

It was this very relationship which taught me, which showed me that there were relationships between men and women that demonstrated the profound equality between the two sexes. I did not consider myself superior to you, or more intelligent, or more active, so that I put myself on the same footing. We were equals. Oddly enough, I think that this increased my *macho* in some way, because it allowed me to rediscover my *macho* with other women, to be full of *macho* again. Yet our equality did not seem to me to be simply the particular equality of two individuals, but to reveal the profound equality of the two sexes.

In any case, you did accept The Second Sex. *It did not change you at all; I must say that it did not change me either, because I think our convictions were the same at that time.*

We had the same convictions—that is, both of us believed that the socialist revolution would necessarily bring about the emancipation of women. We certainly had to sing a different tune later, because we saw that women were not truly equal to men in the U.S.S.R., or in Czechoslovakia, or in any of the so-called socialist countries that we knew about.

Moreover, that is what persuaded me to adopt an openly feminist attitude starting in about 1970. By this I mean a recognition of the specificity of the women's struggle. And you followed me in that direction, but I would like to find out precisely how far. What do you think now about women's struggle for liberation? For instance, how do you think it ties in with the class struggle?

For me they are two struggles with different forms and different directions, so that they do not always overlap. Up to now the class struggle has consisted of men confronting other men. Essentially it involves relations among men, relations tied up with power or economy. Relations between men and women are very different.

Undoubtably there are very important economic implications involved here. But women do not form a class, and in relation to women, men do not either. In other words, for the oppressed there are basically two major lines of battle: the class struggle and the struggle between the sexes. Of course, the two lines often meet.

These days, for example, the class struggle and the struggle between the sexes tend to overlap. I say "tend" because they do not share the same structural principles. The wife of the bourgeois and the wife of the worker are not exactly opposed as classes. The split into bourgeois and working class extends to women only in a very minor way. For example, one often sees cases of relations between a bourgeois woman and her maid that would be unthinkable between the bourgeois factory owner, or an engineer in that factory, and a semiskilled worker in the same factory.

What kind of relations do you mean?

Relations in which the bourgeois woman talks about her husband, about her relations with her husband, about her house. . . . Certain ties can exist between two women of different classes. Except in specific cases where a woman is the head of a business, for example, I don't think a bourgeois woman belongs to the bourgeoisie. She is bourgeois through her husband.

You mean the traditional bourgeois woman?

Yes. First, as a girl, she lives with her parents, under her father's authority. Then she marries a man who will act on the same principles as her father, modifying them slightly.

She does not have an opportunity to assert her place in the masculine class, in the bourgeois class. Of course, in many cases she assimilates bourgeois principles. She often voices the same opinions as her husband, and with even more vehemence. And in her own way she imitates her husband's behavior when she has dealings with "inferiors."

For instance, she is ambivalent toward her maid; she has an ambiguous attitude toward her. They enter into an alliance of sex, a strictly feminine relationship. The bourgeois woman confides in the maid; the maid understands her and is able to account for her trust when she thinks about it a little. On the other hand, there is the bourgeois woman's authority, which she acquires only through her relationship with her husband.

In other words, you would accept the argument put forward by some women in the Women's Liberation Movement, that the bourgeois woman is bourgeois only by proxy.

Certainly, seeing that she never has the same relationship to the economic and social world that a man does. She has this relationship only through an intermediary. Very seldom does a bourgeois woman deal with capital. She is sexually tied to a man who has this relationship.

What is also striking is that if a bourgeois woman is supported by her husband and does not have a father who can take charge of her again if the husband should ask for a divorce, she is forced to look for work. And very often this work will be so badly paid that it hardly keeps her above the level of the proletariat.

I can see what my mother's relation to money was. First she received money from her husband, then from her father. Then she was proposed to by another man, my stepfather, who supported her until his death. At the end of her life she lived partly off what my stepfather had left her and partly off certain sums which I gave her. From the beginning to the end of her life she was supported by men, and she had no direct relation to capital.

In other words, you acknowledge the specificity of the women's struggle?

Absolutely. I do not think it derives from the class struggle.

For me, feminism is one of a number of struggles taking place outside the class struggle but linked to it in some way. There are many others nowadays: the struggles of the Bretons and the Occitanians, for example, which do not overlap with the class struggle.

Still, they are more closely tied to it.

The rebellion of the young soldiers is also something apart from the class struggle. I think many movements today are at one and the same time related to the class struggle and independent of it, or at least incapable of being reduced to that struggle.

They would have to be examined one by one. I admit that the specific character of the women's struggle against men is in no way the struggle of the oppressed classes against their oppressors. It is something else. But the struggle of women against men is certainly in essence a struggle against oppression, since men are trying to confine women to a secondary position.

What importance does the feminist struggle, which you recognize as such, have in your eyes? Would you still hold to the old distinction between primary and secondary contradictions, and would you think that the feminist struggle was secondary?

No, I consider the women's struggle to be primary. For centuries this struggle took place only between individuals, in each household. These individual struggles are beginning to come together and create a more general struggle. It is not reaching everyone. I would even go so far as to say that most women do not realize that they would benefit by adding their individual struggle to a larger struggle, the struggle of all women against all men. This larger movement has not yet reached its peak.

There are some areas in which even women who are not very conscious of their situation feel their interests to be at stake. In the beginning, the battle over abortion was waged by a handful of intellectuals. When we signed the manifesto of the 343, there were still very few of us, but so many women responded to it that we finally managed to push the government into passing the law on abortion. The law is not entirely satisfactory, far from it; but it is still a victory.

Yes, but many men are in favor of abortion too. Often it is the man who pays for the abortion. A married man with a mistress, for example, does not want her to have a child.

I think you're optimistic about the solicitude men feel for pregnant women. There are a great many cases in which the man clears out without giving any money or moral support at all. The fight for abortion was won by women.

Yes, to a certain extent. But after all, it was an assembly of men who passed the law. In this case there was a degree of alliance between the sexes.

In any case, there are many women who are not positively aware of their oppression, who find it natural to do all the domestic work themselves, to care for their children almost completely on their own. What do you think about the problem that members of the Women's Liberation Movement confront when they deal with working class women who are exploited not only in the factories where they work, but also at home by their husbands? Do you think their eyes should be opened to domestic oppression?

Certainly they should. But it is clear that nowadays there is a gap between bourgeois or *petit bourgeois* women and working-class women. They have basically the same interests and they can communicate with one another as women, but they remain separated from one another. That is mainly because of the separation of classes which sets their husbands against one another, and because they are obliged to reflect the ideas about society which their bourgeois or working-class husbands hold. That is what separates the bourgeois woman from the working-class woman most of all. In other respects their lives are much the same—concerned with the management of the home, the care of the children, and so forth.

Yes. But the working-class woman who also has a job is the victim of both kinds of oppression.

My question, then, is precisely this—and I have practical reasons for asking you: should one turn the woman against her husband, when he often seems to her the only refuge from the oppression of her employer?

There is a contradiction in this area. But we must realize that it is the opposite of what people usually say it is. The major contradiction is that of the battle between the sexes, and the minor contradiction is that of the class struggle.

When the woman is subject to two forms of oppression, the battle between the sexes takes priority. I think the working-class woman should create a synthesis, which would vary according to the particular case, between the workers' struggle and the women's struggle, and that she should not minimize either one. I don't think it will be easy, but that is the direction for progress to take.

Yes; but I remember a discussion we had after Karmitz's Coup sur coup. *Members of the Women's Liberation Movement and working-class women were in the audience at the screening. When we spoke of the oppression they suffered*

*at the hands of their husbands, they let it be clearly under-
stood that they felt much closer to a working-class husband
than to a bourgeois woman.*

In some sense that seems obvious to me. But the question is to find out whether the problems faced by bourgeois
women are not the same as those faced by working-class
women. Because, as we have seen, when the bourgeois woman is abandoned by her husband or simply widowed, she
may very well join the working-class woman, or in any case
the *petit bourgeois* woman, in working at very badly paid
jobs.

*A connection between the class struggle and the battle
between the sexes appears in cases where women form movements to improve jobs or working conditions.*

*I know of two examples. There was a strike in Troyes two
or three years ago, and the women leading it said with great
spontaneity and violence to members of the Women's Liberation Movement who were questioning them, "Now that I
understand what it means to rebel, I'm not going to let anyone step on my toes at home any more. My husband is going
to stop pulling rank on me."*

*In the same way, the women employees of the Nouvelles
Galeries in Thionville, who were staging an uncompromis-
ing strike, talked in an extremely feminist way when they explained that they were becoming aware of precisely these
two forms of exploitation, and that they refused to put up
with either one. Then can we conclude that at the risk of
creating a certain degree of rather painful conflict for the
woman, you think it is a good thing to help open her eyes
to her situation?*

Definitely. It seems impossible to me to suppress what is
for part of the people one of the most important struggles
between human beings. Since women are victims, they must
become aware of it.

I agree with you. They must become aware of it, they must find a way of fighting, they must not feel isolated in their fight.

Now there is another question I'd like to ask you which I think is important and which is discussed within the Wo-men's Liberation Movement. What relationship would be established between equality and "promotion"?

On the one hand, we are in favor of an egalitarian society in which not only the exploitation of man by man would be done away with, but also hierarchies, privileges, and so forth. On the other hand, we want to have the same qualifications as men, we want to start off with the same opportunities, have the same salaries, the same chances within a career, the same possibilities of reaching the top of the hierarchy. There is a certain contradiction in this.

The contradiction exists in the first place because there is hierarchy. If, as I hope, a movement arises which is able to do away with this hierarchy, then the contradiction will disappear. That is, women will be treated in exactly the same way as men. There will be a profound equality between men and women, and this problem will cease to exist.

But we must consider things as they are today. Today, men themselves are fairly equal where secondary or low-paid jobs or nonskilled labor is concerned. But there are also very well-paid jobs that demand a certain knowledge and bestow power. I think it would be legitimate not only for the major-ity of women to unite in favor of absolute equality between men and women in a situation where hierarchies shall no longer exist, but also for them to work within the present society to prove, through a few chosen women, that they are the equals of men even in the most elite positions.

I therefore believe that on condition that they belong to the same egalitarian and feminist movement, a certain num-ber of women should—since they can—go to the very top of the social ladder in order to show that they do not lack intelligence when it comes to mathematics or science, for example, as many men claim, and that they are capable of holding the same jobs as men.

It seems to me that for the time being, it is indispensable that there be these two categories of women. As long as it is understood that the elitist category is in some sense delegated by the entire body of women, it is essential to prove that within the society as it now is, based on elitism and injustice, women, like men, can be at the top of the hierarchy. This seems necessary to me, because it would destroy the arguments of the men who are against women and who claim that women are intellectually or otherwise inferior to them.

One might say that it would destroy their arguments but not convince them. They want to think women are inferior because they want to stay on top. But isn't there a risk that these women will be used as excuses? Here, too, there were different feelings within the Women's Liberation Movement on the subject of Mlle Chopinet.* Some, including me, said it was a good thing that she proved her ability. And others replied that men would take it as an excuse to say,, "But you are given the same chances; it is obvious that you can be just as successful as men; so don't say you are being kept in an inferior position." What do you think of this danger?

I think it exists, though it is easy to refute their argument and you have already done so adequately, for example in the issue of *Les Temps modernes* devoted to women. Yet the danger exists. That is why the woman-as-excuse whom you speak of is an ambiguous creature. She can be used to justify inequality and she is only a delegate, in some sense, of the women striving for equality. Yet I think that society

---

* Mlle Chopinet received highest honors at the Ecole Polytechnique.

being the way it is, we can't neglect the fact that there are women who hold men's jobs and succeed just as well as men do.

And then one always runs the risk of serving as an example, of being used as an example by whatever one is fighting against. It comes back to the idea of "playing into their hands . . ." One cannot undertake anything without playing into someone's hands in one way or another. For example, we are not going to stop writing with the excuse that even if we write against the bourgeoisie, the bourgeoisie will claim us as bourgeois writers.

Well, we agree that it is a good thing for women to have the highest qualifications. But I would like to differentiate between two things—qualifications and positions. Because even if they are qualified, are they going to accept positions which we are opposed to?

I think that as things are now, it is impossible to conceive of qualifications which do not lead to positions. . . . Once she occupies these positions, the woman can bring about changes.

What can also be said is that there are positions which men will turn down too. After all, a woman ought to refuse to be an inspector general or a minister in the government as it is now, but a man should too. Basically, the same things that are impossible for one are also impossible for the other. But women risk getting trapped, because they will be exercising the power given them by their qualifications within a world where men have almost all the power.

For example, one might hope that a woman doing biological research would concentrate on female problems— menstruation, contraception, and so forth. Whereas in fact she will do research within areas already established by men. Her position is very delicate, I think, because she should not be serving purely masculine interests.

And this brings us to another question, one that is also much disputed within the Women's Liberation Movement: should women totally reject this masculine universe, or should they make a place for themselves within it? Should they steal the instrument, or change it? I am talking about science just as much as language and the arts. All values bear the stamp of masculinity. Should we completely reject them because of this, start with nothing, and try to re-invent something radically different? Or should we assimilate these values, take them over, and make use of them for feminine ends? What do you think?

That poses the problem of whether or not there are specifically feminine values. I notice, for example, that novels about women often try to enter the interior life of the woman, and that their authors use masculine values to account for what women do. There are some purely feminine values involving nature, the earth, clothes, and so forth, but these are minor values which do not correspond to an eternal feminine reality.

There you are raising another question, that of "femininity." No one among us recognizes the idea that there is such a thing as a feminine nature; but culturally, hasn't the oppressed status of women developed certain defects in them, if also certain good qualities, which are different from those of men?

Definitely. But this does not imply that if feminism triumphs in the near or distant future, these principles and this kind of sensibility will continue to exist.

However, if we believe that we possess certain positive qualities, wouldn't it be better to communicate these qualities to men, rather than try to eradicate them from women?

It is actually possible that women have a better, more interior, more precise self-knowledge than men do.

If, as you said in the beginning, you prefer to be with women than with men, isn't it because, through their very oppression, they have avoided certain masculine defects? You have often said that they were not as "comical" as men.

That's certainly true. Oppression has a lot to do with it.

What I mean by "less comical" is that when a man considers himself to be an average man, he encounters external conditions which make him truly comical.

For example, when I described my *macho* as a personal quality and not the effect of the social world on me, I was comical.

Do you mean that a man is more easily fooled?

More easily fooled and more often comical. The society of men is a comical society.

To put it simplistically, because each one assumes various roles and is completely stilted in his roles?

That's right. The woman, as an oppressed person, is almost more free, in a way, than the man is. She has fewer principles dictating her behavior. She has more disrespect.

Then you would say that you approve of the feminist struggle?

Absolutely. And I find it entirely normal that the feminists do not agree with one another on certain points and that there are arguments and divisions. This is normal for a group at the point where you are. I also think they lack a broad base of support in the masses and that their work now should be to gain it. If that were achieved, and if the feminist struggle maintained its ties with the class struggle, it could shake society in a way that would completely overturn it.

On The Idiot of
the Family

*You have been working on Flaubert for a very long time.
Could you describe the different stages of your work to us?
Tell us in particular why the publication of your study was
delayed until now.*

JEAN-PAUL SARTRE   You already know from *The Words*
that I read Flaubert in my childhood. I read him again more
closely in the Ecole normale, and I remember going back to
Sentimental Education in the thirties. I have always had a
kind of animosity toward Flaubert's characters. It is because
he puts himself inside them, and since he is both a sadist and
a masochist, he shows them to us as miserable and unsympa-
thetic people. Emma is stupid and mean, and the other
characters are hardly any better, except Charles—who em-
bodies one of the author's ideals, as I eventually discovered.

The moment when I truly confronted Flaubert was during the Occupation, when I read the correspondence in four
volumes edited by Charpentier. At that time I found the
man himself unpleasant, but discovered that certain aspects
of the correspondence illuminated the novels for me. After
some reflection, I said to myself in 1943 that I would cer-

Interview with Michel Contat and Michel Rybalka, published in Le
Monde, *May 14, 1971.*

tainly write a book on Flaubert some day. In fact, I announced this in *Being and Nothingness*, at the end of the chapter on existential psychoanalysis.

I made no secret of my antipathy for Flaubert in *What Is Literature?* But I hardly thought about him between 1943 and 1954; I had other books to write then. Around 1954, during the period when I was close to the Communist Party, Roger Garaudy suggested to me, "Let's take someone and try to explain him—I will do it by Marxist methods and you by existentialist methods." He thought I would approach things in a subjective manner and he would approach them objectively. The idea of a comparison therefore came from him, but I was the one who chose Flaubert. I was thinking of *Madame Bovary*, a book Flaubert always hated, and one which brought him both unexpected fame and notoriety.

In three months I filled twelve notebooks. What I did was both rapid and superficial, but I was already using psychoanalytic and Marxist methods. I showed the notebooks to Pontalis, who had just written a study of Flaubert's illness, and he said to me, "Why don't you turn this into a book?" I went to work and produced a study of about a thousand pages, but abandoned it around 1955. Some time afterwards, I told myself that I couldn't go on abandoning my projects in the middle. (*Being and Nothingness* promised a study of ethics that was never written; the *Critique of Dialectical Reason* ends after the first volume; the study of Tintoretto was interrupted in the middle; and so on.) I decided that for once in my life I would have to finish something. I have continued to feel this need, this resolve to carry through to the very end. The *Flaubert* has kept me busy for ten years, and though naturally I had other things to do, I can say that after I finished *The Condemned of Altona*, I worked on nothing else. Part of *The Words* was already written. In 1963 I needed only three months to revise the first version and remove the somewhat too ironical tone I had given it. Thus my study went through three or four versions before the present one, which was totally rewritten between 1968 and 1970. The first two volumes are being published now; I think there will be two more.

As to the delay you mention, it was simply due to a desire to deepen the study and introduce new elements.

You once said that the Critique of Dialectical Reason *could have been better written, more compactly organized. Like Marx, it seems that you don't have the time to "be brief." Are you satisfied with the form of your study?*

I can see several factual errors as I leaf through the book: for example, Flaubert's father wrote a treatise on *physiology*, not philosophy; toward the end it was Elbehnon, the character from Mallarmé's *Igitur*, that I should have been talking about; and so on.

As far as the form goes, I wanted the style of the *Flaubert* to be exactly the way it is, because I didn't want to go to any trouble. Books like this should be written without letting stylistic worries predominate. Flaubert is the one who has style; if one wrote with style about an author whose whole life was devoted to a search for style, it would be madness. Why waste time composing beautiful sentences? My aim is to show a method and to show a man.

The book was written straight out: the simplest, most easygoing form is the best. If stylistic effects sometimes appear, it is because certain difficult or "unsayable" things cannot be expressed in any other way.

There is a sense of style in *The Words* because the book is a farewell to literature: an object that questions itself must be written as well as possible. If the *Flaubert* resembles *The Words* in places, it is because after fifty years of writing one winds up being impregnated with one's own style and because certain turns of phrase come spontaneously, without any effort.

Even though I have done nothing else for several years, I have enjoyed writing the *Flaubert* and never felt that it was a burden. On the other hand, I no longer have any opinion whatsoever about the book; I am too much inside it and too much outside it. And what is more important, I am at an intermediate stage with it, a stage of half limbo, between the two finished volumes and what remains to be written. I am not troubled by this, because I am sure I will be able to finish the *Flaubert*. Since the end of October I have hardly written a line: it is the first time I have taken a six-month rest since before the war.

It seems that as you wrote The Idiot of the Family *you were hoping to do two things: on the one hand, to write a novelistic work which in spite of its innovations could be linked to the nineteenth-century tradition of the* Bildungs-roman; *on the other hand, to do a study which by its rigorous character would be a scientific model.*

I would like my study to be read as a novel because it really is the story of an apprenticeship that led to the failure of an entire life. At the same time, I would like it to be read with the idea in mind that it is true, that it is a *true* novel.

Throughout the book, Flaubert is presented the way I imagine him to have been, but since I used what I think were rigorous methods, this should also be Flaubert as he really is, as he really was. At each moment in this study I had to use my imagination.

Is it really a question here of imagination? Isn't it rather an intelligence capable of relating the various elements to one another?

Intelligence, imagination, sensibility are one and the same thing for me and can be described by the word "experience" [*vécu*]. I am obliged to use my imagination: if, for example, I take a letter from 1838 and another from 1852, no connection was ever made between these documents by Flaubert, by the correspondents, or by the critics. At that time the connection did not exist. When I make it, I make it with my imagination. And once I have imagined it, this can give me a real connection.

But do you consider The Idiot of the Family *to be a scientific work?*

No. And it is for that reason that I had the book published in the Philosophical Library series. "Scientific" would imply rigorous *concepts*. As a philosopher I try to be rigorous with *notions*. The way I differentiate between concepts and notions is this: A concept is a way of defining things from the outside, and it is atemporal. A notion, as I see it, is a way of defining things from the inside, and it includes not only the time of the object about which we have a notion, but also its own time of knowledge. In other words, it is a thought that carries time within itself. Therefore, when you study a man and his life, you can only proceed through notions. For example, if you formed a concept of passivity—which is so important with Flaubert—it would no longer mean anything because it would have been made into something exterior. If you want to take it as a historical whole, you must show where it comes from and how it develops (Flaubert's passivity while writing *Madame Bovary* was not, of course, the same as that of a nursing baby). In addition, it is necessary to see how the very notion of passivity is discovered and how thought—my thought, in this case—takes hold of it and develops it. You therefore have two temporal elements: the beginnings and development of passivity, with the method that tries to deal with it, and at the same time, interiority, that is to say, ideas which overlap with one another, which have internally negative—or dialectical—relationships. All that is included in the idea of a notion. The distinction I make between concept and notion is similar to the distinction I make between knowledge and understanding. The attitude necessary for understanding a man is empathy.

That is the attitude you have toward Gustave, but not toward his parents. . . .

Let's be fair: I am not very extreme in my attack on the parents. I believe they made Flaubert what he was—that is to say, someone who was unhappy and who found a neurotic solution to this unhappiness. Therefore I allow the greater part of the responsibility to rest with them. But it is not true that I do not like the father, Achille-Cléophas. Although the documents are lacking, one can sense the presence of qualities in him which one would like to know more about, and which show that he was different from what one would normally expect: his relation to his memories, for example, and the fact that he used to cry—tears probably being a heritage of the revolutionary sensibility of the eighteenth century. (Rousseau used to cry, Diderot used to cry, everyone at that time used to cry a great deal.) For all that, and also for the hours he spent dissecting cadavers, I rather like him. And finally, he was professionally inventive, unlike his son Achille, who did hardly more than apply his father's methods. But it is true that I don't like Flaubert's mother.

That's clear. And one sometimes has the feeling that you are using your discussion of the Flauberts—the parents and especially the mother—to settle your own scores with this family, with all bourgeois families.

A little with all families. In my book there is undoubtedly a constant attack on the bourgeoisie of the period, of which the Flaubert family was typical. Concerning my dislike for Flaubert's mother, it would be a mistake to infer that it is my own mother I am discussing through her. My mother was not only devoted, but full of tenderness. The child whose portrait I implicitly draw in contrast to the young Gustave— the little boy who is sure of himself, who has profound convictions because in his first years he had all the love that a child needs in order to become an individual and a self that dares to affirm itself—that little boy is me. From this point of view I am the complete opposite of Flaubert. I really hold a grudge against Caroline because I myself was well loved.

If you like, I am taking a different point of view here from that of an analyst, who would say, "We are studying Flaubert; we will consider his family as it is—objectively, coldly, and so on—and we will see how this child created his difficulties from objective structures." Now I myself think that the family had a harmful effect, that the father was abusive, that the mother was frustrating and almost totally without affection—which was the source of Flaubert's autistic tendencies—and that the older son unintentionally provoked in Gustave a jealousy which in a certain sense destroyed him. I have insisted on this aspect of the relationship between the two brothers because it is often neglected by the biographers, Thibaudet in particular. And yet all you have to do is read Flaubert's juvenilia attentively to discover that they are filled with themes which show the very poor relationship between the two brothers.

Your study is based to a large degree on the writings of Flaubert's youth. Did you analyze them in order to corroborate your first intuitions?

No. It was in reading these writings that I discovered many things—for example, Flaubert's sexuality. I had only to interpret them. Confirmation came to me later, quite recently, in the unedited passages of letters dating from the trip to the Orient, passages which were censored in the Conard edition. Along with his homosexual tendencies, what appears most strongly is the passive character of his sexuality. I laid great stress on the notion of passivity, which is not a category that belongs in classical psychoanalysis and which pediatricians, as I learned in my conversations with them, do not take very seriously. For them passivity is only the effect of a conatus, a natural tendency, while I believe that in the case of Flaubert it has two causes: the way he was handled while being nursed by a mother who felt little love for him, and the crisis that occurred over his learning to read at the age of seven, when his father took charge in an authoritarian and repressive manner, using blackmail in the name of family honor. The example of the reading progress of his older brother, Achille, was held up as a family model to Gustave and gave him a feeling of inferiority, a feeling that his older brother could not be equaled, which only reinforced his original passivity. From this point of view, Flaubert seems destined for passivity by his very position as a younger brother.

Destined? This might shock those who see you as the philosopher of freedom!

In a certain sense, all our lives are predestined from the moment we are born. We are destined for a certain type of action from the beginning by the situation of the family and the society at any given moment. It is certain, for example, that a young Algerian born in 1935 was destined to make war. In some cases history condemns one in advance. Predestination is what replaces determinism for me. I believe we are not free—at least not these days, not for the moment—because we are all alienated. We are lost during childhood. Methods of education, the parent-child relationship, and so on, are what create the self, but it's a lost self. It is obvious, however, that there is an enormous variation between different kinds of alienation: take, for example, autistic children or wolf children. . . .

I do not mean to say that this sort of predestination precludes all choice, but one knows that in choosing, one will not attain what one has chosen. It is what I call the necessity of freedom. For example, Flaubert was not completely conditioned to choose writing. It came little by little, starting when he began to learn how to read. All this corresponds to the part of the *Critique of Dialectical Reason* in which I describe the nature of alienated freedom. In fact, Flaubert himself said: "I do not feel free." Familial constraints exercised a rigorous conditioning on him. In a family of scientists he was denied the possibility of becoming a scientist, because the older son was the one to inherit his father's position. Everything was played out in advance: options remained for Gustave, but they were conditional options. This is what I show in my book.

According to Lacan, the self is an imaginary construction, a fiction that is identified after the fact. This is what he calls the mirror stage, or an identification with the character created by the society and family. Now your description of the Flaubertian self seems to correspond completely to Lacan's theory, but you describe it as something specific to Flaubert, whereas for Lacan it is universal.

I was not thinking of Lacan when I described Flaubert's make-up—to tell the truth, I do not know Lacan's work very well—but my description is not far from his conceptions. I do not present the formation of the person as specific to Flaubert, but as something that applies to us all. And the formation consists in fact of creating a person with roles and an expected kind of behavior, based on what I call the constituted being. In other words, it would be necessary to do the same work on everyone—on very active people too— as I have done on Flaubert. The task would be to show the formation and the personalization of the individual, that is to say, how he moves toward the concrete from the abstract conditioning of the family structures. It is certain that with Flaubert the element of unreality is all-embracing. The difference between Flaubert and other people in whom imaginary elements obviously cannot help appearing—is that Flaubert wanted to be *totally* imaginary.

You know how I conceive of the self—I haven't changed: it is an object before us. That is to say, the self appears to our reflection when it unifies the reflected consciousnesses.

Thus there is a pole of reflection that I call the self, the transcendent self, which is a quasi object. Flaubert *wants* his self to be imaginary.

How do you see Flaubert's neurosis?

My analysis of his neurosis was a kind of antipsychiatry: I wanted to show neurosis as the solution to a problem.

Up to this point we have discussed only psychoanalytic themes. At what moment in your research were you obliged to use Marxist methods based on precise historical knowledge?

From the very beginning I used both methods. I feel that it is impossible to speak of a child or a young man without situating him in his time. If Flaubert had been the son of a surgeon fifty years later, his relationship to science would obviously have been different. Likewise, the ideology he was taught from childhood on must be described. Therefore the two methods are both necessary. However, properly speaking, the first two volumes of my work make use of empathy in order to show how the child interiorizes the social world. But that is not all there is to it: the third volume will show in what way Flaubert's neurosis is a neurosis *required* by what I call the objective spirit. In other words, though I do not think that art or literature must necessarily be the result of neurosis—even though artists are often neurotic—I think that the idea of art for art's sake does depend on neurosis. A useful study—and this is what I am doing in the third volume, which I plan to publish in two or three years—would be the history of the artistic movement around 1850. It will use as examples several writers, including the Goncourts, and especially Leconte de Lisle. These writers are all more or less neurotic. In the first two volumes I seem to be showing Flaubert as inventing the idea of art for art's sake because of his personal conflicts. In reality, he invented it because the history of the objective spirit led someone who wanted to write in the period 1835 to 1840 to take the neurotic position of post-romanticism, that is to say, the position of art for art's sake.

What are the greatest difficulties you have encountered in your research?

I believe the greatest difficulty was introducing the idea of the imagination as the central determining factor in a person. As it stands now, the book is connected with *Imagination*, which I wrote before the war. But what I try to do with the *Flaubert* is also to use the methods of historical materialism, so that when I speak of words, I am referring to their materiality. I feel that speaking is a material fact—just as thinking is, what's more. I have rethought some of the notions dealt with in *Imagination*. But in spite of the criticism I have read, I must say I still consider that work to be sound. If one takes only the point of view of the imagination (excluding the social viewpoint, for example) I have not changed my position. It would obviously be necessary to take up the subject again from a more materialist point of view.

Another difficulty was to succeed in this method through empathy. I was often opposed to Flaubert in the past; little by little, however, that disappeared. Now I tell myself that I wouldn't like to have dinner with him because he would be extremely boring, but I can regard him as a man.

Empathy, then, presupposes that you suspend all moral judgment?

Of course. That was what was needed for a work like this. If I judged Flaubert by a system of values, I would still remain very close to my old judgment. Perhaps I can no longer judge him because he suffered too much—too much and too little at the same time, for as you know, he imagined his own sufferings somewhat—but he really was an unhappy man. And then, for me, the fact that Flaubert said "dirty worker" does not have any bearing on the present, because the fascists do not say "dirty worker"; they say "The workers are with us." This distance is another reason why I was able to achieve empathy.

To what extent did you use in the Flaubert *the tools that you created in the* Critique of Dialectical Reason?

I did not have to use them much in the first volumes, but I will call upon them in the third because in it there will be collectives, serialities. I will have to speak of the objective spirit and so on. This will be the moment for totalization by Marxist methods.

Is it because this totalization is possible for the nineteenth century and not for our time that you have not tried to elucidate yourself as you did Flaubert?

To some extent, yes. But another reason is that I do not have any empathy for myself. There is always a little sympathy or antipathy in one's relations with oneself. But empathy can only be addressed to someone else. One is loyal to oneself. This excellent expression was used by a handwriting analyst: she had described a woman's personality and the woman said she was flattering her enormously. The analyst replied: "But that is because you are loyal to yourself. I am telling you things that I think are accurate, and you find them favorable; that is because you want to. It does not in the least mean that according to other criteria they would be so favorable." I think that one can make an effort to become detached from oneself and move toward objectivity and empathy. But we consider certain things in ourselves to be "valuable" which in reality, seen from another point of view, may be blemishes, faults, weaknesses. Therefore I do not think that one can understand oneself through empathy. For example, *The Words* did not work that way at all.

However, as far as the dates go, there is some connection between the project of your autobiography and the Flaubert project. Didn't the discovery of Flaubert's neurosis correspond somewhat to the discovery of your own neurosis?

No. I do not think it is very helpful to say that I see myself in Flaubert as it has been said that I do in Genet. Perhaps it is more nearly true for Genet because he is closer to me in many respects. But I have very little in common with Flaubert. One of the reasons I chose him was precisely because he is not close to me. One always says about a writer describing someone, "In painting the other he paints himself." Of course, there must be elements of myself in the book, but the essential thing is the method.

Was it out of the question to try to use this method on yourself—for example, to analyze your own early writings or your correspondence?

If I found all the letters I wrote in my twenties, and if I wanted to amuse myself by studying *Jésus la Chouette* or stories from that period in detail, I would certainly discover aspects of myself that I was not aware of. In fact, it does happen that when I reread texts of mine, I see things that strike me as having previously escaped me—I mean places where I have revealed myself in spite of myself. Thus empathy is always possible, but it has limitations. I do not think it would be very interesting to do this work on myself. There are other ways of looking for oneself. Maurice Merleau-Ponty once said to me that he wanted to write about himself, about his life, in an autobiographical form. A little later he said, "No, it would really be better if I wrote a novel. Why? Because in a novel I could give an imaginary meaning to the periods of my life that I don't understand." You might say it is similar to the problem of self-analysis. It is considered possible, but it is not scientific. Likewise, if I try to study myself, assumptions will inevitably enter the picture because of my loyalty, or my adherence, to myself.

When you say this, aren't you saying that what you called

pure or nonaccessory reflection in Being and Nothingness—
which is a requirement for authenticity—is impossible?

You know that I never described this kind of reflection;
I said it could exist, but I only showed examples of accessory
reflection. And later I discovered that nonaccessory reflection
was not different from the accessory and immediate way of
looking at things but was the critical work one can do on
oneself during one's entire life, through *praxis.*

Finally, there is an additional reason having to do with
the totalizing method itself: it is impossible to totalize a
living man. The method may be chronological, but it is
always prepared to illuminate the chronology by referring to
the future. To show Flaubert's false generosity, for instance,
I use two examples that are widely separated in time: Gustave's relationship with his sister Caroline during their childhood, and Flaubert's last friendship, with Laporte around
1875. These two examples illuminate one another. But I can
do this because Flaubert's life is a completed totality. What
I did in *Saint Genet,* for example, was much less complete.
Living writers hide themselves: when one writes, one dis-
guises oneself.

*Aren't you a little afraid of the idea that someone might
try to elucidate you as you did Flaubert?*

On the contrary, I would be happy. Like all writers, I hide
myself. But I am also a public man and people can think what
they like about me, even if it is severe. Not all writers are
equally calm about this. For instance, when Genet held in his
hands the manuscript of my book about him, his first impulse
was to throw it in the fire.

You are not afraid of the judgment of posterity?

Not at all. And it's not that I am convinced it will be
favorable. But I do hope this judgment is made. And it
wouldn't occur to me to get rid of letters and documents

concerning my private life. All that will be known. So much
the better if this means I will be as transparent to posterity—
if it takes an interest in me—as Flaubert is to me.

*Isn't this desire to read Flaubert like an open book—in
just the way that the Creator reads his creatures—the project
of a demiurge, a way of trying to become God?*

Not at all. The most important project in the *Flaubert*
is to show that fundamentally everything can be communi-
cated, that without being God, but simply as a man like any
other, one can manage to understand another man perfectly,
if one has access to all the necessary elements. I can deal
with Flaubert, I know him; and that is my goal, to prove that
every man is perfectly knowable as long as one uses the appropriate method and as long as the necessary documents are
available. I do not claim that my method is the definitive one.
There could be quite a few methods different from mine,
though close in spirit.

*Suppose that nothing remained of Flaubert for us but
Madame Bovary. Would the aim of your research still have
been to reconstruct Flaubert the individual, this hypotheti-
cal object? Or rather, like a good many contemporary critics,
wouldn't it have been necessary for you to abandon the idea
of the man behind the work, to let the creator subject
vanish, and concentrate not on the individual but on the
text, in the sense that semioticians use this word today?*

I am completely opposed to the idea of the text, and that
is precisely why I chose Flaubert. By leaving us juvenilia and
an abundant correspondence, he offers us the equivalent of
a "psychoanalytic discourse." Also, I happen to know the
nineteenth century very well, so that I can show the importance of social factors in the formation and personalization of Flaubert the individual who wrote *Madame
Bovary*. . . .

But one could answer you that these days there is no

longer any question that the experiences of childhood and the
social conditions of a period are the necessary conditions of
the work produced by the adult writer. One could argue that
it is therefore not this incontestable causality that should be
studied, but rather the unique configurations of a particular
text.

In order to study these configurations, it is necessary to
begin with a study of the socioeconomic, ideological, and ana-
lytic conditions, among others. For example, Flaubert wrote
Saint Antoine first, and then *Madame Bovary* several years
later. There was only one person who saw that they had the
same subject, and that was Baudelaire. No one made this
assertion again, no one showed that *Madame Bovary* is a cosmic novel. If you want to understand the relationship between
the two works, it is necessary to see what Flaubert thought
after the failure of *Saint Antoine*—when Bouilhet claimed
that it should be thrown down the toilet. It is necessary to
see Flaubert reflecting on it during his trip to the Orient with
Maxime du Camp and to see him then taking up his subject
again and centering it around a sixteenth-century girl who
lives with her family and becomes a saint through a series of
events. There are already elements in this that begin to relate
it to *Madame Bovary*. Then Flaubert takes up yet another
theme and at last, one day, *Madame Bovary* emerges. One
sees that what he was trying to do was precisely to evolve a
cosmic knowledge—and in the case of *Saint Antoine* it was in
a sense very banal—from a random story. He understood at
that moment that one can tell a story about anything as long
as a totalization is brought about.

How can you expect to see all that if you do not know the
kind of crisis which followed *Saint Antoine* and made him
write *Madame Bovary*? It is impossible to study it without
going back to the person, that is to say, to the study of the
documents which reveal him to us. Obviously that's not always possible, but if there are no documents at all, you find

yourself in the same situation as the anthropologist who tries to study a vanished people: the object does not exist! Only hypothetico-deductive sciences, like mathematics, can begin with nothing—that is to say, with the mind. I want to elucidate the relationship between the man and the work. With Flaubert the connection was easy. In his correspondence he is just as open as if he were lying on the analyst's couch— unlike George Sand, for example, who constantly hides herself in her correspondence. With her, writing functions like censorship; with Flaubert, it is the reverse: when you have the correspondence in fourteen volumes, you have the man himself. For another writer, you would have to change the method a little. Let's take George Sand again: the letters would have to be checked against each other, as well as verified by the testimony of her correspondents or friends. It would be more difficult, but it would still be possible.

As we study *Madame Bovary*, what we discover right away is defeat. That is to say, we discover a man with a destiny, who was lost in his childhood, who has to a certain extent found himself again, but not very successfully, and who consequently inscribes his defeat in a book. But a book is not only a defeat; it is also a victory. It must therefore be shown how the book as victory demands another author than the unhappy Flaubert whom I describe in the first volumes—the Flaubert who has projected himself into his book. There is no a priori reason for his book to be good: it could have been the work of a madman. Thus there is another Flaubert. Yet in reality there is only one, and he oscillates constantly between the two poles of defeat and victory. When I study his life I can only find the defeated Flaubert, and when I study *Madame Bovary* I must discover what the victorious Flaubert is.

In other words, a moment comes in the research when the *text* must be confronted: that is the moment of victory. When I come to *Madame Bovary*, I will of course find elements of defeat. For example, there are the numerous passive verbs, which often account for the flaw in Flaubertian sentences and which are partly responsible for causing Flaubert's work to be what Malraux called "beautiful and paralyzed novels." From this point of view, the style represents the failures that I explain in the first volumes by referring back to Flaubert the person, using my methods. This does not change the fact that the work is a success which has been handed down to posterity independent of its author. This success must be accounted for. I want to do a totalizing critique: that is why the last volume will be a textual or "literary" study of *Madame Bovary*, and in it I will try to use "structuralist" techniques.

Are these techniques compatible with your methods?

I think so, if they are adapted. But it is too early to say. I only "know" my book up to the third volume, which is partly written. I will get back to it in October. I suppose that it will take me three years; one year to finish the neurosis, that is, to show how it was required by the style, and then two years for *Madame Bovary*. To a certain extent, *Madame Bovary* is already implied by *The Idiot of the Family*, but it interests me to the extent that it is not implied by *The Idiot*, and it will lead me to use new techniques, to come back finally to the portrait.

Are you familiar with the current research influenced by formalism and rhetoric?

Yes. I have just read Bakhtine on Dostoyevski, for example, and I don't see what the new formalism—semiotics —has added to the old. On the whole, what I object to in these studies is that they don't lead to anything. They do not embrace their object; the knowledge dissipates itself.

Over the course of the fifteen years you have been working on the Flaubert, *you nevertheless must have had to readjust some of your ideas in the light of contemporary research.*

It is true that I have assimilated certain ideas through indirect reading, as in the case of Lacan. In the same way, I found in about 1939 that I had assimilated many things from Hegel, though I didn't know his work well. I did not really come into contact with Hegel until after the war, with Hippolyte's translation and commentary. In fact, I rarely undertake very methodical reading; it is more or less chance that decides. I am sent nearly everything and I read what interests me. Whether it is *Critique,* or *Tel quel,* or *Poétique,* I read it. But I feel that *Critique* is less interesting today than it was ten years ago. The linguists want to treat language as exteriority and the structuralists who come out of linguistics also treat totality as exteriority. For them, this means taking the concepts as far as possible. But I can't do this because I do not place myself on a scientific level but on a philosophical level, and that is why I don't need to exteriorize what is total.

In other words, in order to disagree with you, it is necessary to reject you completely?

I think so, and this is true for most philosophers.

What is new about the notion of experience [vécu] *that you often substitute now for what you used to call consciousness?*

I suppose it represents for me the equivalent of conscious-unconscious, which is to say that I no longer believe in certain forms of the unconscious even though Lacan's conception of the unconscious is more interesting. . . . I want to give the idea of a whole whose surface is completely conscious, while the rest is opaque to this consciousness and, without being part of the unconscious, is hidden from you. When I show how Flaubert did not know himself and how at the same time he understood himself admirably, I am indicating what I call experience [*vécu*]—that is to say, life aware of itself, without implying any thetic knowledge or consciousness. This notion of experience is a tool I use, but one which I have not yet theorized. I will do that soon. I suppose that with Flaubert, experience is when he speaks of the illuminations he has had which then leave him in the dark, so that he can't find his way. He is in the dark before and after, but there is a moment in which he has seen or understood something about himself.

How do you see the relationship between Flaubert and language, the problem of what he called the "unsayable"?

The whole relationship of Flaubert to language, the priority given to spoken language over written language, was something I did not discover until recently. What Flaubert calls the "unsayable" is, in fact, what he does not want to say but what he *knows*—for example, his feelings toward his father and his brother. And it is also what we mean today by the inexpressible. I show in the book how Flaubert at first believed that "poetry" could not exteriorize itself into a poem, but that it was a way of life which the words betrayed. During this period he always said: "There are no words to render the beauty of a woman or the aroma of a plum pudding." Afterwards he discovered an imaginary use of language that was capable of rendering imaginary things. From that moment on he found in a totality the possibility of making the beauty of a woman or the aroma of a pudding felt in the imagination. But he postulates nevertheless the incommunicability of experience. The theme of incommunicability, as we know, is one of the major themes of the nineteenth- and early-twentieth-century bourgeoisie. It has in fact produced important works. Flaubert himself was led to the idea of incommunicability because, owing to his protohistory, the use of affirmative language was not available to him. It is therefore not completely the same. It goes without saying that I am absolutely opposed to Flaubert's conceptions and that in my book I am only describing them. I hope no one will be mistaken about this.

Several times before, you had talked about Flaubert's "total disengagement" and in Search for a Method *you speak of his "literary engagement." What connection do you see between these two ideas?*

Total disengagement is what appears on the surface of everything he wrote. But one can then observe an engagement on another level, which in spite of everything I would call a political level. It is a question here, for example, of the man who could insult the Communards, a man who was a landowner and a reactionary. But to stop there would not be fair to Flaubert. To grasp him truly, one must go to the deepest engagement, the engagement by which he tried to save his life. The important thing was that Flaubert was deeply engaged on a certain level, even if this implied that all the other positions he took were reprehensible. Literary engagement is in the end the act of taking on the entire world, the totality. Poulet has remarked on the theme of circularity in Flaubert, but he has not gone far enough and has not realized that his circularity is totalization. To take the universe as a whole, with man inside, to become aware of it from the point of view of nothingness, is a profound engagement, and not merely a literary engagement in the sense that one "is engaged in making books." Flaubert—like Mallarmé, who was his spiritual grandson—felt a true passion, in the Biblical sense.

Speaking of this, is there any connection between your unpublished study on Mallarmé and The Idiot of the Family?

The study on Mallarmé—which I have lost, by the way —was much less systematic than the *Flaubert* and much closer to *Saint Genet.* This connection is obvious because I constantly need to refer to Mallarmé and to symbolism in order to understand Flaubert better.

Why, in the end, did you prefer to write the Flaubert

instead of the second volume of the Critique of Dialectical Reason?

This second volume requires an enormous amount of reading, and I do not know if I will have the time to do it before I die. Of course, I could limit myself to one point in history, and that is doubtless what I will do if I write the book.

Could you see forming a group of researchers who could work on the second volume under your direction?

That hardly seems possible to me, since I would have to do all the reading myself. For the *Flaubert* I had some help in getting hold of several documents, but this help was not essential.

At the moment, I understand, you are thinking of two other projects: a play on a historical subject and a political testament in an autobiographical form.

I am vaguely thinking about it. I should write a play now, for various reasons, but I don't feel like doing a play, so that idea bores me stiff. . . . As for the testament, I know that it will be written, but I have not yet written a line, and I don't know when I will do it.

For the moment I have only one assignment, and it is a pleasant one: to finish the *Flaubert*.

How will this program fulfill the literary project that you have had since childhood?

As you know, what happened to most of the people who, like me, were born around 1905 was that they reflected, or interiorized, a certain society and that there were then two breaks. One occurred in 1914–1918, and the other, which was much more complete, in 1945. We have therefore found ourselves with a different project. Everything originates in childhood, but in one sense my current project no longer has anything to do with the one I had at the age of twelve or fifteen, when I wanted to be a novelist and was influenced by the idea of art for art's sake, vaguely tinted with my grandfather's humanism.

You hardly see anything more than a "mini-praxis" in literature today.

Yes. But anyway, there is no more literature!

You said before that The Words *was your farewell to literature. In a certain sense, couldn't* The Idiot of the Family *be considered as a return to literature?*

That's the same question my leftist friends ask me all the time. To the extent that the *Flaubert* is a novel, it ties in with what I used to write before. But to the extent that I am trying to develop a method that is more or less revolutionary—because it is Marxist—it is linked to my new problems.

There is certainly something ambiguous here, and I felt it while composing the book. On the one hand, the fact that I deal with someone from the nineteenth century and am concerned with what he did on June 18, 1838, can be called an escape. On the other hand, my aim is to propose a method on which another method can be constructed, and that, in my opinion, is contemporary. Also, when I look at the content, I have the impression that I am escaping—and perhaps this is somewhat the case—and when, on the other hand, I look at the method, I have the feeling that I am of the moment. There are two aspects to this, one of which is the development of the method, and the other of which is an escape. Perhaps that is one of the reasons why I was able to achieve empathy. Having said this, I am certain that if I were fifty today, I would not begin the *Flaubert*.

You would agitate?

Agitate? . . . There are more interesting ways of using

your pen for the leftists—for example, in a popular tribunal or in *J'accuse.* . . .

I am not entirely satisfied with these political texts because they do not go far enough. But that is the practical problem, which I have not yet resolved very well: how can a political writer make himself understood by a popular audience while carrying out an idea to the very end?

In my opinion the new style of intellectual must give everything to the people today. I am sure one can go far in this direction, but I do not yet know how. In any case, this is one of the things I am looking for.

It is also clear that the leftists are not very preoccupied by theory. What interests them—even the intellectuals among them—is to discuss an action that has been carried out and to draw lessons from it or to discuss another action still to be carried out.

It has recently been suggested to you several times that you write a novel which would serve the cause of the revolution.

Yes, but I don't see the need, and I do not feel the need within myself. There are so many things left for me to do.

POLITICAL
ESSAYS

The Burgos Trial

If the press is to be believed, the Burgos trial caused such a scandal only because it exposed the absurd ferocity of the Franco regime. I do not believe this is true; does fascist savagery really need to be demonstrated? Since 1936, have there not been imprisonments, tortures, and executions almost everywhere on the soil of the Iberian peninsula? The trial disturbed the consciences of people in Spain and outside Spain because it revealed to those who had not been aware of it the existence of the Basque nation. It was clearly apparent that this existence, while singular in itself, is far from being the only case of its kind, and that large nations contain colonies within their borders. At Burgos the defendants were chained and, for all practical purposes, gagged. But at the cost of an unremitting battle, they brought the idea of centralization to trial.

Thunder in Europe: to take only one example, French children are taught that French history is nothing other than the unification of all "our" provinces, begun under the kings, continued by the French Revolution, and completed in the nineteenth century. It was important, I was told in school, to be proud of this. National unity, which was accomplished

Preface to Proces de Burgos *by Gisèle Halimi, Éditions Gallimard, 1971.*

by us at an early date, explained the perfection of our language and the universality of our culture. Whatever our political points of view, it was forbidden to question this. On the issue of unity, socialists and communists found themselves in agreement with the conservatives: they considered themselves to be the inheritors of Jacobin centralism and, reformists and revolutionaries alike, they wanted to bring the benefits of the new regime to France as an indivisible whole.

Today, no one is concerned about the fact that monarchical absolutism was born from the development of roads and means of communication, the appearance of the cannon, and the "mercantilist" demands of merchant capital. The Revolution and Jacobinism allowed the bourgeoisie in power to pursue the unification of the economy by destroying the last feudal and ethnic barriers and by winning foreign wars through large-scale forced conscription of all the inhabitants old enough to carry arms, regardless of their ethnic origin. The nineteenth century eliminated piecework [*le job*] through industrialization and its consequences—the rural exodus, the integration of enterprises, and the new ideology of bourgeois nationalism. The present unity is, in the end, the result of a secular project on the part of the currently dominant class. This class has attempted to produce everywhere—from Bidassoa to the Belgian border—the same type of abstract man, defined by the same formal rights (for this is democracy!) and the same real obligations without taking into account his concrete needs. That is simply the way it is, and no one is going to interfere with it.

Hence the shock of December 1970. The trial was disgraceful and absurd, but could the charges brought against the prisoners be contested without at the same time admitting the validity of at least some of the objectives of the E.T.A. [the Independence Party]? Of course, the Spanish government is openly fascist, and that confused things a bit. What the majority of the protestors were attacking with a clear conscience was the Franco regime. But it was also necessary to support the accused, and wasn't the E.T.A. saying: "We are not only fighting against Francoism, we are fighting above all against Spain"? That was the hard pill to swallow. How could it be admitted that the Basque nation existed on the other side of the Pyrenees without recognizing the right of "our" Basques to become part of it? And then what about Brittany? And Occitania? And Alsace? Would the whole history of France have to be re-written upside-down, as Morvan-Lebesque recently suggested, and would Du Guesclin, the hero of centralism, have to be considered simply as a traitor to the Breton cause?

The Burgos trial called attention to a new fact: the re-emergence more or less everywhere of what central governments are in the habit of calling "separatist" tendencies. In the U.S.S.R. many of the republics, most notably the Ukraine, are feeling the effects of centrifugal forces. It was not so long ago that Sicily seceded. In Yugoslavia, France, Spain, Northern Ireland, Belgium, Canada, and many other places, social conflicts have an ethnic dimension; "provinces" discover themselves to be nations and more or less openly demand national status. One begins to understand that the present borders correspond to the interests of the dominant classes and not to popular aspirations, that behind the unity which is such a source of pride to the great powers is oppression of ethnic groups and the hidden or open use of repressive violence.

There are two clear reasons for the present strengthening of national movements. In the first place, they were given impetus by the atomic revolution. Morvan-Lebesque reports that an autonomist leader in Brittany, after learning about the Hiroshima explosion, cried out: "At last the Breton problem exists!" Indeed, before that, the idea of central unification was justified and supported by pointing to the threat of hostile neighbors. With the advent of atomic weapons this blackmail no longer holds: the centralism of the cold war emanates from Moscow and Washington and affects nations, not provinces. Now, as these nations worry about belonging to one of the two blocs, other smaller nations, which were formerly assumed to be integrated, become conscious of their own independent existence.

I think the second reason for the strengthening of national movements, which is related to the first, lies in the process of decolonization which began on three continents after the last World War. Imagine a young man born in the Finistère going to do his military service in Magreb around 1960. He has been told that he is to take part in a simple police action to put down the crazy and illegal agitation taking place in several overseas French departments. But now the French are defeated; they withdraw the departmental division, leave Algeria, and recognize its sovereign national status. For the demobilized soldier, what does it mean to be an inhabitant of the Finistère? In Algiers he saw that the departments were abstract divisions which concealed a history of forceful conquest and colonization. Why wouldn't it be the same on the other side of the Mediterranean, in what is called the "mother country"? The Finistère —which really exists only for the administration—disappears into abstraction before the eyes of the young man. He feels himself to be Breton, nothing more, nothing less, and French only by right of conquest. Will he resign himself to being colonized? If he is tempted to revolt, the example of the Algerians and the Vietnamese is there to encourage him. The victories of Vietnam, in particular, teach him that the colonists have skillfully limited the field of possibilities for him and his brothers. He has been inculcated with defeatism. As a Frenchman, he has been told, everything is open to him because he has the right to vote, just like a Beauceron. As a Breton, he could not even lift a finger, let alone rise up against the central power, which would crush him in an instant. But in Indochina, a few million peasants drove the French into the sea and are now fighting victoriously against the greatest military superpower of the capitalist world: that, too, was "impossible." Well, evidently it is not. Suddenly the field of his possibilities is enlarged. Could it be that the colonizing powers are no more than paper tigers?

The splitting of the atom and decolonization, then, are what lead to a new feeling of patriotism among conquered ethnic groups. Actually, everyone knows this, but many people in France, Spain, and Canada believe that the desire for independence among ethnic groups is only a whim inspired by false analogies, and that such separatist movements will die out by themselves. Now the example of the Basque country shows us that this rebirth is not a passing phenomenon, but something necessary. It would not even have taken place if the so-called provinces had not had a national existence all along which for centuries others tried to take away from them and which, though suppressed and obscured by their conquerors, remained there as the fundamental and historical link among their inhabitants. It would not have taken place if the existence of this link, tacitly recognized by the central power, did not explain the inferior situation of the conquered ethnic group within the country of the conqueror and, as a consequence, the ferocious struggle for self-determination waged by the group.

The existence of the Basque nation, whose *necessity* was asserted at Burgos, continues to help the Catalans, the Bretons, the Galicians, and the Occitanians to deal with the question of their own destiny. Here, I would like to try to contrast the abstract universality of bourgeois humanism and the singular universality of the Basque people. I will attempt to show the circumstances which have led this people by an ineluctable dialectic to produce a revolutionary movement. And I will examine the theoretical consequences that we can reasonably infer from the present situation—that is, the profound transformations which decentralization can help bring about in the thinking of centralized socialism.

If we refer to history without centralist prejudice, it becomes clear that the Basque ethnic group is in every way different from the neighboring ethnic groups. It has never lost the awareness of its singularity, which is marked *in every case* by biological characteristics that have been kept intact until today, and by the fact that Euzkara, its language, cannot be placed in the family of Indo-European languages. As long ago as the seventh century, the duchy of Vasconia comprised a population of mountain people who defeated the armies of Charlemagne at Roncevaux. This duchy was transformed around the year 1000 into the kingdom of Navarre, which began to decline at the beginning of the twelfth century and which was annexed by Spain in 1515. In spite of the conquest, and undoubtedly because of it too, Basque consciousness—or the consciousness of being Basque —was strengthened.

At this time the feudal era was hardly over, and Spanish centralization was still in its early stages. Spain allowed the defeated people to keep certain rights they had possessed in in the Middle Ages—the *fueros*, which would long remain the bastion of Basque resistance and which were defended by the entire people. The fact that the people were not satisfied with this relative autonomy, that they champed at the bit and did not lose hope of recovering their independence, is proved by the unsuccessful proposition made by a deputy from Biscay to Napoleon at the time when Napoleon was remaking Europe: to create within the empire an independent Basque state.

The rest is well known. The constitution of 1812 virtually suppressed the *fueros*, and the nationalist movement went astray in a blind attempt to resurrect the past. In opposition to Isabella II, who was more liberal but still a centralist in the French manner, the popular forces defended the absolutist pretender to the throne, Don Carlos (another traditionalist, but one who, out of love for the past, wanted to give Navarre back its feudal autonomy). Two wars, two defeats. In 1879 Euzkadi lost its last privileges and sank into a sanctimonious traditionalism that turned its back on history. It came to life again six years later when Sabin Mana founded the P.N.B. (the Basque Nationalist Party), whose active members were mainly bourgeois and intellectuals. There was no longer any question of agitating for absolutism in the hope of regaining the *fueros*. Rather, the P.N.B., which was politically progressive (because it demanded independence) and socially conservative, remained traditionalist in part, as one of its slogans proves: "Old laws and sovereignty."

At this point Basque resistance made some impression on the Spanish, several of whom—such as the anarchist Pi y Margall—proposed a federalist solution to the problems of the peninsula. Later, in the time of the republic, the project was taken up again, and the central government agreed to recognize the principle of regional autonomy provided that it was approved in a referendum by 70 percent of the populations concerned. Upper Navarre, which was essentially rural and therefore attached to Carlism (the Carlists would soon be fighting on Franco's side) voted against autonomy.* The other three provinces voted yes by an enormous majority. The republican government, which was more centralist than it seemed, showed bad faith by allowing things to drag on until 1936. Finally it was forced to recognize autonomy by the pressure of events and for essentially practical, even military, reasons. It was a question of winning over the Basque country and being assured that the population would resist Franco's putsch by armed struggle.

The Basque government was immediately established. It contained three socialists, two liberals, and one communist, which shows both that the influence of the P.N.B. extended to the most diverse levels of society and that it had somewhat modified its original conservatism. Until April 1937 the Basque troops ferociously defended Guipuzcoa and

---

* It is clear that they were rejecting not autonomy but the Republic.

Biscay. What followed is well known: Franco sent in reinforcements, began a reign of terror, and bombed Guernica! There were 1,500 dead; by the month of August the republic of Euzkadi had come to an end. After the war, repression followed: imprisonments, tortures, executions. President Aguirra, head of the P.N.B., sought refuge in France. During the Second World War he supported the democracies, hoping that the fall of Hitler and Mussolini would be followed by that of Franco. Today we can see the full extent of our shame and his naïveté.

The P.N.B. had played out its role: since 1945 it has been in steady decline. In 1947, however—no doubt with the intention of forcing the Allies' hand—it unleashed a general strike. The Allies did not make a move, and allowed Franco to crush the strike with pitiless repression. That was the end: in Euzkadi the party maintained a certain prestige because it was the "historic" party which remained at the origin of the ephemeral Basque republic. But it could no longer take action: its methods were no longer relevant to the situation. The exiles grew old; Aguirra died. It didn't matter: we will soon see how the E.T.A. came forward at the right moment to replace the old bourgeois party. This brief survey is enough to show how Euzkadi, an ethnic group only *recently* conquered by Spain, has always ferociously refused to be integrated. If the Basques were allowed to vote today, I leave it to the imagination to conceive how overwhelming the majority would be in favor of independence.

However, can we accept the E.T.A.'s claim that Euzkadi is a colony of Spain? This is an important question, for it is in the colonies that the class struggle and the struggle for national independence merge. Now, in the colonial system, the colonized countries furnish raw materials and food products at a good price to the industrialized mother country: this is because labor is underpaid. But we must point out that the Basque country, particularly in the provinces of Guipuzcoa and Biscay, has been fully developed industrially since the beginning of the century. In 1960 the annual consumption of electric energy per person was 2,088 kilowatts in the two provinces, compared with 650 kilowatts for Spain and Catalonia.* The annual steel production per person is 860 kilograms in Biscay, 450 in Euzkadi, and 45 in Spain-Catalonia. The distribution of the working population in Guipuzcoa is as follows: workers in primary activities, 9.45 percent; secondary activities, 56.80 percent; tertiary activities, 33.75 percent.† In Biscay the same distribution is 8.60 percent, 57.50 percent, and 33.90 percent. In Spain-Catalonia, on the other hand, it is 43.50 percent, 27.20 percent, and 29.30 percent.

The considerable size of the work force in Guipuzcoa and Biscay that is employed in secondary and tertiary activities, combined with the fact that in these provinces the rural population is in constant decline, shows the enormous effort on the part of the Basque country to develop industry. Guipuzcoa and Biscay are from this point of view the pilot regions of the entire Iberian peninsula. Thus if a colonial situation did exist, one would encounter the paradox that the colonizing country is poor and predominantly agricultural while the colonized country is rich, with a demographic profile comparable to that of industrialized societies.

On closer inspection, however, this paradox is an illusion. Euzkadi might be prosperous, but its population is only two million. In 1515 there were far fewer people and the population was rural. The conquest was possible because the two countries had a homogeneous structure, and one of them was much more densely populated than the other. On the other side of Bidassoa, lower Navarre was systematically pil-

---

* Spain and Catalonia are so distinct from one another in every way that it is inappropriate to use common statistics, but the official reports that we refer to confuse them intentionally. It goes without saying that if we were furnished with figures for Spain alone, they would be much lower.

† Primary activities: work involved with raw materials, such as mining and agriculture. Secondary activities: factory work, manufacturing. Tertiary activities: service work, such as transportation, civil service, etc. [Translators' note.]

laged, laid waste, and depopulated by the conquering French: the colonization is more evident. It is clear that the lethargy of Spain during the first thirty years of the century allowed southern Euzkadi to develop a flourishing *regional* economy centered around the economic pole of Bilbao. But *who* profits from this economy? That is the question. One can give a half-hearted answer by saying that there is no conquered country which does not pay tribute to its conqueror. But it is more reliable to consult the official records.

The records inform us that Spain engages in a veritable financial pillaging of the Basque country. The tax policy crushes the workers; taxes in Guipuzcoa are higher than anywhere on the whole peninsula. On top of this, in *all* the provinces that it considers *Spanish*, the government spends more than it receives in taxes: 150 percent in Toledo, 151 percent in Burgos, 164 percent in Avila, and so on. The two industrialized provinces of the Basque country* pay to the *foreign* government that exploits them 4.3384 billion pesetas, while in Euzkadi the Spanish government spends only 774 million pesetas.† Thus it steals more than 3 billion pesetas to maintain the Castilian desert. In addition, most of the 774 million that is "given back" goes to instruments of oppression (a Spanish or Spanish-influenced administration, an army of occupation, police, courts, etc.) or to instruments of de-Basquification (in the university, only Spanish language and culture are taught).

Now, the problem of Basque industry is above all a problem of productivity. For prices to be competitive on the world market, modern machines must be imported. The Spanish state, which is partially autarchic, is opposed to this. Credit from Madrid is discriminatory and favors Castile at the expense of Biscay. In order for Bilbao and Pasajes to adapt to maritime traffic and accommodate high-tonnage

---

* In Navarre the Spanish government gives back 106 percent.

† These particular figures are for one of the years between 1960 and 1970, but the statistics are noticeably constant from one year to the next.

ships, they must be given new equipment. The work would be considerable, as would the work of reclaiming the fishing ports. Nothing has been done. Even the railroad network, previously installed by the Spanish, is a great handicap: to go by train from Bilbao to Vitoria one must travel 137 kilometers; on the highway the distance is 66. But the administration and the I.N.I. (the National Institute of Industry), an organ of the oppressor state, are run by ignorant and fussy bureaucrats who know nothing of the needs of the country (in part because they consider it a Spanish province, at least theoretically) and block indispensable improvements.

Spain reserves the right to absorb noncompetitive products. She plays the political game of taxes, but in reverse: by preventing certain costs from being lowered, she gives herself the right to consume Basque products without increasing the producer's benefits. The consequences are inevitable: the per capita revenue is one of the highest on the peninsula, which doesn't mean anything; and the revenue of salaried workers (who form 85 percent of the active population) is much lower than that of the inhabitants of Madrid, Burgos, Valencia, and the rest. It should also be pointed out that the rate of salary increases from 1955 to 1967 was 6.3 percent for Spain and 4.15 percent for Euzkadi.

Thus in spite of the extensive industrialization of the region, we find two essential components of classic colonization: pillage—financial or other—of the colonized country, and overexploitation of the workers. To that is added a third, which is merely a consequence of the first two: the rhythm of emigration and immigration. The Spanish government has profited from the needs of industrialization by sending the unemployed from poorer regions to Euzkadi. They have been promised advantages (for example, they have priority for housing) but, overexploited like the Basques and without a developed class consciousness, they constitute for management a mass of unskilled laborers. There are 300,000 to 351,000 immigrants among a population of 1,800,000 to

2,000,000. Conversely, the Basques from the poor regions emigrate. Especially those from Navarre: there are 150,000 to 200,000 Basques in Madrid, of which around 100,000 are Navarrese. The extent of this emigration causes a drain, and the arrival of Spanish workers in industrial regions can be considered as the beginning of colonial deconstruction.

Such a consistent political tactic on the part of the Franco regime obviously implies the complicity of the most powerful management groups in Biscay and Guipuzcoa. In fact, the latter have been centralists and liberals since the time of the Carlist wars, when the haute bourgeoisie appeared in Bilboa. In the last few years the head offices of large enterprises have begun emigrating to Madrid. The most powerful elements among the bourgeoisie see nothing but advantages to be gained from putting a halt to modernization through Spain's incompetence and autarchy. The vast Spanish market absorbs products that are noncompetitive at the international level, and the owner is assured of a high percentage of profit without being obliged to make large investments. Working against the true interests of the nation, these "collaborators," whose centralism will end by ruining the Basque economy, voluntarily remain apart from the community and play the role (classic in itself) of those who are called *compradores*. In the final analysis, within the structure of a centralizing system, they profit by a kind of Malthusianism.

The conclusion is clear: in spite of appearances, the situation of a Basque wage earner is very similar to that of a colonized worker. He is not simply exploited—as a Castilian is, for example, who is engaged in a "pure" class struggle— but deliberately overexploited, since his salary is lower than that of a Spaniard doing the same work. There is an over-exploitation *of the country* by the central government with the complicity of the compradores, who exploit the workers by means of this system of overexploitation. Overexploitation does not benefit the Basque capitalists, who are simple exploiters, overburdened by taxes and protected by a foreign army. It benefits only Spain, that is, a fascist society supported by American imperialism.

Nevertheless, the working classes are not always conscious of the overexploitation. Many wage earners thought even recently of associating themselves with the demands and actions of the Madrid and Burgos workers, which would have led them to a negative centralism. It was necessary to make them understand that in the case of Euzkadi, the economic and social question had to be stated in national terms. When the country no longer paid financial tribute to the occupier, when its true problems were formulated and solved in Bilbao and Pamplona rather than in Madrid, it could freely transform its economic structures at the same time.

For, it must be repeated, the Spanish overexploit the Basques *because they are Basques*. Without ever admitting it officially, they are convinced that the Basques are *other*, both ethnically and culturally. Does anyone think they have forgotten the Carlist wars, the 1936 Republic, the 1947 strikes? If they hadn't remembered, would they make such violent efforts to destroy the Basque language? Clearly it is a question of colonial practices. For a hundred years the French struggled to destroy the Arab language in Algeria; if they were not completely successful, they at least turned literary Arabic into a dead language that is no longer taught. They did the same thing, with varying success, to Euzkara in lower Navarre and to Breton in Brittany.

Thus attempts are made on both sides of the border to convince an entire ethnic group that its language is nothing more than a dialect in the process of disappearing. In southern Euzkadi its use is practically forbidden. The establishment of *iskatolas* [primary schools taught in Basque] is prohibited, Euzkara publications have begun to be eliminated, the schools and the university teach the language and culture of the oppressor. Radio, motion pictures, television, and the newspapers explain the problems of Spain in Spanish and propagandize for the Madrid government. The administrative personnel is Spanish or Spanish-oriented, recruited through competitive examinations given *in Spanish* by Madrid functionaries. Because the foreigners wanted it so, in Bilbao it is said with bitterness: "Basque language and culture are not good for anything." And the inspired press willingly repeats an unfortunate statement by Miguel de Unamuno: "The Basque language will soon be dead." That is not all: In the schools boys are punished if they speak Basque. In the villages the peasants are allowed to speak Euzkara, but they must not attempt to do so in the city. One of the Burgos defendants had authorization to receive visits from his father in prison. This authorization was withdrawn when it was learned that the father spoke to him only in Basque—not, of course, in order to provoke an incident, but because he did not know any other language.

The forcible suppression of the Basque language is an act of true cultural genocide. Basque is one of the oldest languages in Europe. To be sure, it appeared at a time when the economy of the whole continent was rural, and if it did not later adapt easily to the evolution of society, it was because the conquering Spanish forbade its use. To become a twentieth-century language (which it already is to some extent), all that is needed is for people to speak it. Hebrew in Israel and Breton in Quimper encountered the same difficulties, and these difficulties were resolved. Today, Israelis who discuss data processing or atomic fission can read the manuscripts of the Dead Sea scrolls as we would read Racine or Corneille. And Morvan-Lebesque observes that Breton has more regularly formed words to designate modern realities than French, the "national" language. The resources of an old language that has remained young because it has not been allowed to develop are considerable. If Basque were reinstated as the national idiom of Euzkadi, it would carry with it, through its own structures, all the richness of the past and a specific way of thinking and feeling that would open itself fully to the present and the future. But what the Spaniard wants to do away with is the Basque personality. In Biscay, to *make oneself Basque* is in effect to speak Euzkara. Not only does a person thereby recapture a past that belongs only to him, but even when he is alone he is addressing the community of people who speak Basque.

At Burgos the last statements of the "accused" were made in Euzkara. As they challenged the Spanish court that claimed to be judging them without even understanding them, they summoned their entire people into the room. At that moment they were all there, invisible. The official transcript notes at this point that the defendants made unintelligible remarks in a language "that seemed to be Basque." A wonderful euphemism: the judges understood nothing, but they knew perfectly well what it was all about. To avoid seeming to recognize that the nation of Vasconia had invaded the Tribunal, they reduced Basque only to a *probable* language, so perfectly obscure that one never knew if the speaker was really speaking or if he was simply uttering sounds without meaning. This, then, is the core of Euzkadi culture and the greatest worry of the oppressors. If they manage to destroy this language, the Basque will become the abstract man they want him to be and will speak Spanish, which is not and never has been *his* language. But as this will not put an end to his overexploitation, he has only to become aware of colonization for Euzkara to be revived. Naturally, the reverse is also true: for a colonized man, to speak his own language is already a revolutionary act.

The Basques of developed consciousness today go even farther in defining the culture they are given and the one they want to give themselves. Culture, they say, is the creation of man by man. But they quickly add that there will not be a universal culture as long as universal oppression has not been destroyed. Official culture in Euzkadi today is universalist in that it wants to make of the Basque a universal man, devoid of all national idiosyncrasy, an abstract citizen in every way similar to a Spaniard, except that he is overexploited and does not know it. In this sense, there is no universality except that of oppression. But men, no matter how oppressed they may be, do not become *things*. They become, on the contrary, the negation of the contradictions that are imposed on them. Not primarily by force of will, but because they naturally contain within themselves a surpassing of themselves and a project [*dépassement et projet*]. Thus we have the Basques—who *at first* cannot help being the negation of the Spanish man that has been put into each one of them. It is not an abstract negation but a living negation, embodied in all that they find to be singular in themselves and their environment.

In this sense, Basque culture today must be first of all a counterculture. It is created by destroying Spanish culture, by rejecting the universalist humanism of the central powers, by making a constant and mighty effort to reclaim Basque reality. This reality is right before their eyes—for it is the landscape, the ecology, and the ethnic traits as well as Euzkara literature—at the same time that it is travestied by the oppressor in an innocent and outdated folklore for foreign tourists. That is why they add this third element: Basque culture is the *praxis* which emerges from the oppression of man by man in the Basque country. The *praxis* is not immediately self-conscious and willed. It is the daily effort, directly provoked by the intake of official culture, to rediscover the concrete—that is to say, not man in general, but the Basque man. And this work, conversely, must result in a political *praxis*, because the Basque man cannot affirm himself in his fullness except in his *own* country that has once again become sovereign.

Thus by an inexorable dialectic, conquest, centralization, and overexploitation have had the result of both keeping alive and frustrating the Euzkadi demand for independence by the very efforts Spain has made to suppress it. At the present time we can attempt to determine the precise need of this concrete situation, that is, the nature of the struggle it requires from the Basque people today. There exist two types of Basque response to Spanish oppression, and both are inadequate. To give these substance and form, we will say that one is the response of the Euzkadi Communist Party and the other that of the P.N.B.

To the Communist Party, Euzkadi is simply a geographical name. The party receives its orders from Madrid, from the Spanish Communist Party, and does not take the local situation into account. Thus it remains centralist, meaning that it is socially progressive and politically conservative; it hopes to lead the Basque workers toward a "pure" class struggle. To do this is to forget the problems of a colonized, that is to say, overexploited, country. In spite of several opportunistic declarations in favor of the E.T.A. during the Burgos trial, the party does not understand that the actions it is proposing have inadequate objectives and are therefore without real weight. If the Basques began to struggle against exploitation pure and simple, they would be abandoning their own problems in order to help the Spanish workers in overthrowing the Francoist bourgeoisie. They would be renouncing what is Basque in themselves and limiting themselves to demanding a socialist society for the abstract and universal man, who is a product of centralizing capitalism. And when this man takes power in Madrid, when he controls the instruments of work, will the Basques be able to count on his gratitude to *grant* them autonomy? Nothing is more doubtful. The republic, it was seen, needed considerable coaxing, and the socialist countries today do not hesitate to engage in colonialism.

The Basques can only fight *alone* against overexploitation and the denial of Basque culture. This does not mean that they will not have tactical alliances with other revolutionary movements when it is a question of weakening Franco's dictatorship. But strategically, it is impossible for them to accept a common direction. Their struggle will take place in isolation because they are waging it against Spain (not against the Spanish people); a colonized nation cannot put an end to overexploitation except by rising up independently against the colonizer.

On the other hand, the P.N.B. is wrong to consider independence as an end in itself. "First of all let us form a Basque republic," they say. "Then we will see if we have to improve our society." If by any remote chance they did manage to create a Basque state on the bourgeois model, it is true that overexploitation would come to an end. But it would not take very long for this state to fall under the influence of American capitalism. As long as the society retained a capitalistic structure, it is safe to assume that the compradores would sell themselves to the highest bidder. Foreign capital would submerge the country, the United States would govern through the intermediary of the local bourgeoisie, neocolonialism would succeed colonialism, and overexploitation, all the more efficiently masked, would continue as before. Only a socialist society, because it rigorously controls its own economy, can establish economic relations with both capitalist and socialist nations, and it cannot do so without great risks.*

The inadequacy of these responses by the Communist Party and the P.N.B. shows that independence and socialism are two sides of the same coin. The struggle for independence and the struggle for socialism must be one and the same. If this is so, logically it is the working class—which, as we have seen, is far and away the largest class—that must lead the fight. As he becomes conscious of his overexploitation, and thus of his nationality, the manual worker at the same time understands his socialist vocation. Has the Basque worker already done so? That is a completely different question, and we will speak about it later. On the other hand, large

* To emphasize the importance of these difficulties, I would cite the single example of the relations between Cuba and the U.S.S.R.

portions of the middle classes in a colonized country refuse cultural depersonalization, although they do not always realize the social consequences of this refusal. For in principle, they are the allies of the proletariat. A revolutionary movement conscious of its task in a colony must not be moved by the principle of "class against class," which has meaning only in the mother country. The colonial movement must accept the inclusion of the *petite bourgeoisie* and the intellectuals, on the condition that the revolutionaries from the middle classes place themselves under the authority of the working class. We can see that the first work to be done consists of bringing about a twofold and steadily growing awareness: the proletariat must become conscious of its colonized condition, and the other classes, which are more naturally nationalistic, must understand that for a colonized nation, socialism is the only possible path to sovereignty.

These are the reasons that the E.T.A., or Independence Party, has been able to evolve over the past one hundred and fifty years. It has changed its membership and transformed its backward-looking desire for a return to the *fueros* within the structure of an absolutist state into the forward-looking call for the construction of a sovereign and socialist state. And there is another reason for its evolution which is peculiar to the Iberian peninsula, and which gives a special character to the Basque struggle. In Spain as in Italy and Germany, central unification was not really completed until the twentieth century. As a consequence it took the form of fascist dictatorship, which led to naked and senseless violence in response to the "separatists." In two of these three countries fascism is no longer in power, but Franco has remained the caudillo of Spain. A Basque once said in my company: "We have the horrible luck to have Francoism." Horrible, yes; but why "luck"? If the Spanish regime were a bourgeois democracy, the situation would be more ambiguous: the government would stall, and with false promises and delays it would postpone "reforms" indefinitely. That would un-

doubtedly be enough to create among Basques a large reformist faction which would be the ally of the oppressor
government and would expect nothing more than to be
granted federal status. But since 1937, the blind brutality
of Francoism has proved the foolishness of the reformist
illusion. To each demand expressed today, there is only
one response: violent repression. How can anyone be surprised by it, since the regime was created in order to act in
just this way? But it must be added that a repressive regime
is the *truth* of colonizing Spain. Whatever the form of
Spanish government, we know that centralized Spain deeply
rejects Basque "separatism" and that it is ready, when necessary, to drown any Euzkadi revolt in blood.

The Spanish, to the extent that they themselves are the
products of centralizing idealism, are abstract men. They
believe that except for a handful of agitators, the people in
the rest of the peninsula are too. Do they believe this in
good faith? Of course not; they know that Euzkadi exists,
but want to hide it from themselves. They become outraged
when the Basques assert themselves, and they go so far as to
hate them because they are Basques, that is to say, because
they are concrete men. On a more serious level, the men in
power are not unaware of the fact that the end of the colonial
regime in Euzkadi would quickly lead to increased misery in
Castile and Andalusia. So that as a last recourse, even a
republic would continue to carry out what Francoism started.
The "luck" that the Franco government represents for the
Basques lies in the fact that it shows most candidly the true
nature of colonialism. The government does not argue; it
either oppresses or kills. Since repressive violence is inevitable, there is no other solution for the colonized country
but to oppose violence with violence. The reformist tempta-
tion being out of the question, the Basque people can only
radicalize themselves. They know that at present, independence can be obtained only by armed struggle.

On this point the Burgos trial is clear, for in confronting

the Spanish, the "accused" were aware of the risks: imprisonment, torture, capital punishment. They were not fighting
in the hope of quickly throwing the oppressors out, but in
order to contribute to the formation of a clandestine army.
If the P.N.B. is now in decline, it is because the organization
understood that in the face of fascist troops the Basques had
no other solution but a people's war. Independence or death:
these words, which were recently spoken in Cuba and Algeria, are now being repeated in Euzkadi. Armed struggle for
an independent and socialist Euzkadi is what the present
situation demands. It is either that or submission—which
is impossible.

From 1947 to 1959 this need remained empty and form-
less: to all appearances nothing was being done about it. In
fact, however, it had affected the entire Basque population,
especially the young people, and by 1953 everything had
begun. E.K.I.N., which was founded that year, was a group
of intellectuals who were still hardly conscious of the real
Basque problem in all its tragic simplicity, but who understood the necessity of initiating new and radical action. This
group was soon obliged to enter the P.N.B. which, though
paralyzed, was still powerful. Nevertheless, the E.K.I.N.
distinguished itself from the P.N.B. by its extremist positions. Soon one of its members was excluded from the P.N.B.
for "communism," which led the entire group to stand behind him and leave the nationalist party. This experience
convinced them that the struggle undertaken by the old
party, which had achieved results in 1936, had become pure
rhetoric by the end of the war, with the betrayal of the bourgeois democracies.

In 1959 the group which had founded the E.K.I.N. became the core of a new party, the present E.T.A. In the
beginning, even before it had taken a theoretical position,
the E.T.A. examined the two tendencies that were dividing
the country: the demand for independence and the workers'
revolt. Since 1960 it has understood that in daily practice

these two struggles must be interconnected, each clarified by the other, and jointly led by the same organizations. It was a question of identifying the needs of the present situation slowly but surely, and in a *practical* way. That it has proceeded correctly is proved by the violent crises of the sixties: its "humanist" right wing quit; the "universalist" left was excluded after attempting to abandon the anticolonialist struggle and lead a "pure" class struggle with the Spanish workers. The resignations and departures define its position better than a hundred theoretical writings could have done. After these purges, the E.T.A. in 1968 began to try, in spite of everything, to define itself theoretically. At this level its principles are already fixed. They were developed in the internal struggle of the group against its right wing and a certain centralist left, and in fact they are nothing more than the gradually discovered necessities of the situation.

The E.T.A. has thus organized four fronts: the workers' front, the cultural front, the political front, and the military front—which all function together under a common leadership but remain distinct from one another. In 1969 on the workers' front, the struggle consisted of approaching manual workers, who are often reticent, and of organizing an avant-garde core within the working class. On the cultural front, the E.T.A. led an attack against "the weakest link," which was the dehumanizing universalism of the government of oppression. It has already created *iskatolas*—nursery and primary schools, in which the instruction is exclusively in Basque and which 15,000 children attended in 1968–1969. It has launched a literacy campaign for adults. It has created student committees that are actively demanding (through demonstrations, strikes, and sit-ins) the creation of a Basque university. These committees have also sent Basque artists (writers, singers, painters, and sculptors) right into the villages to give exhibitions and to stage performances of popular songs and street theater. Since 1966 it has organized social schools in which Marxism-Leninism is taught to workers.

On the political front, which is closely tied to the military front, the E.T.A. is politicizing the entire Basque people by showing them the scandal of repression.

The program of politicization explains the current direction of the armed struggle, which does not yet propose to drive out the oppressor, but to mobilize the Basques little by little to form a clandestine army of liberation.* The present tactic can be described as a spiral containing successive stages: action, repression, action. Each action brings on a more savage repression, which exposes the centralizing fascism, which in turn opens the eyes of larger and larger areas of the population and thus makes wider action possible the next time. One can find no better example of this kind of struggle than the dialectical process that has come to a temporary conclusion at the Burgos trial. From the beginning to the end of the process, the E.T.A. imposed its methods and came out ahead. This is what demonstrates the value of its tactics.

At the very beginning, however, these tactics had not been developed. After the massacres of 1936 and the repression of 1937, the heavy peace of the Franco regime fell on the Basque country and crushed it. Against this repressive oppression, the P.N.B. organized an action—the 1947 strike. The strike, which led to no real gains, brought about a terrible repression that resulted in discrediting the P.N.B. But it is precisely because of this failure that the new generation took over, understanding the need to move on to armed struggle. In 1961 the E.T.A. marked its existence with its first action of a military type: home-made bombs went off nearly everywhere, and there was an attempt to sabotage a rail convoy. The second enterprise failed owing to lack of

* However, since August 1970 some members have advocated a partial demilitarization of the E.T.A. in favor of political action by the Basque workers. According to the militants of this tendency, total militarization must be absolutely clandestine and therefore runs the risk of isolating the organization from the working masses and ultimately going against the desired goal.

experience, but it brought about a brutal repression: the arrest of 130 militants. Thus the infernal cycle of action, repression, action was inaugurated. For several years, however, the "forces of order" were frustrated; the E.T.A. was too elusive, and bombing attempts continued all over the region. It was not until the spring of 1968 that the chief of police could publish a communiqué in the Bilbao press stating, "War has been declared against the E.T.A."

The manhunt began, but it did not prevent a bomb explosion a few days later on the highway, causing damage which blocked the route of the cyclists competing in the Tour of Spain. ("Let them pass somewhere else; they have nothing to do with us.") In June a member of the Guardia Civil was found dead on the road. Several hours later, other members of the Guardia Civil fired without cause on a "suspect" and killed him. It was Javier Echebarrieta, one of the leaders of the E.T.A. Repression quickly spread from the clandestine organization to the population at large. By outlawing the celebration of masses in memory of Echebarrieta, the administration in one fell swoop aroused the indignation of the village priests and antagonized the people of the countryside. Since then the increased repression has called forth reactions that have animated the people in the deepest sense. Three months later, Manzanas of the police, a sinister figure well known to the Basques, a man who had tortured people in Euzkadi for thirty years, was executed in front of his apartment door. As predicted, this action loosed a savage repression.

It had come to the point where the government of oppression was now opposed to the entire Basque people. The government could not accept the liquidation of *its* representatives; it would be forced to find the guilty parties, bring them to trial, and demand several executions. But since the "victim" had been an executioner himself, the majority of the people of the country could not resent his liquidation, which was nothing more than a just punishment. The powers fell into a contradiction from which they have still found no escape. From their point of view, which cannot be changed, intimidation must take the form of retribution. But the publicity of the trial showed everyone that this retribution was no more than a parody of justice; the defendants were chosen either at random from prisoners in the jails or, in an effort to undermine the strength of the E.T.A., from those who were thought to be E.T.A. leaders.

Under these conditions the proceedings could only be a farce. There was absolutely no proof against Izco, who was nevertheless sentenced to death. The court was military, even though several of the "accused" had already been sentenced for the same or similar acts in a civil court. The judges were army officers totally ignorant of the law, except for one, who was there to give legal advice to the military men. The lawyers, constantly threatened with prison by the presiding judge, could hardly make themselves heard. The "accused" were chained to one another and, calm and contemptuous, fought without pause, not to defend themselves against the accusations of their oppressors, but to reveal before the journalists the tortures they had been subjected to. The presiding judge, when he was able to quiet them, inevitably answered with a *"No interesa."* It became obvious to the press that these military men had come together not to judge but to kill, after following an absurd ritual that they were not even familiar with. The "charged" finally exposed the repressive violence of Spain by forbidding their lawyers to defend them.

They had won: their admirable courage and the obtuse stupidity of their "judges" had, in the end, turned their trial into a national affair for all Basques. When the workers went on strike in large enterprises at Bilbao, the E.T.A. had concrete proof that it had reached wide areas of the working class. And indignation was so great in the rest of the world that for the first time the Basque question was brought before international public opinion. The Basques of Euzkadi became known everywhere as a martyred people struggling for national independence. A final action, born from repression: the general wrath made Spain back down; the death sentences were commuted. The E.T.A., through a success that was both unhoped-for and necessary to its tactics, had asserted itself as the wheeling flank of the working class in its country. It had gained prestige throughout the mobilized country, prestige as great as that of the P.N.B. twenty-five years before. Its militants are fully aware that the struggle will be long, that it will take, according to them, "twenty or thirty years to put together the popular army." No matter how long it might take, the first shot had been fired at Burgos between December 1970 and January 1971.

This is how things stand: we, the French, who are still in some sense the descendants of the Jacobins even if we do not want to be, have been given a glimpse of *another* kind of socialism by a heroic people led by a revolutionary party. The socialism of the E.T.A. is decentralistic in concept; such is the singular universality that the Basques and the E.T.A. justly oppose to the abstract centralism of the oppressors. Can this socialism be useful to us? Is it not a temporary solution for colonized countries? Stated in other terms, can we see it as an ultimate end, or as a step toward the moment when universal exploitation has come to a close and all men will participate on equal terms in a true universality, through a common overcoming of all singularity? That is the problem for the colonists. One can be sure that colonized people, struggling for their independence, are not worried about this. What is certain in the eyes of the Basque militants is that the right of peoples to self-determination, asserted in its most radical necessity, implies a general revision of present borders. These borders are left over from bourgeois expansion and no longer correspond at all to popular needs. Such a revision can come about only through a cultural revolution which creates the socialist man on the basis of his land, his language, and even his re-emergent customs. It is only in this way that man will little by little cease to be the product of his product and become at last the son of man.

Should we call these conceptions Marxist? We can note some hesitation on that point by the leaders of the E.T.A., since some of them call themselves neo-marxists and others —the majority, it seems—Marxist-Leninists. It is the day-by-day experience of the struggle that will decide. Guevara said to me once: "Are we Marxists? I don't know at all." And then he added, with a smile: "It's not our fault if *reality* is Marxist." What the E.T.A. reveals to us is the need of *all* men, even centralists, to reaffirm their particularities against abstract universality. To listen to the voices of the Basques, the Bretons, the Occitanians, and to struggle beside them so that they may affirm their concrete singularity, is to fight for ourselves as well—to fight as Frenchmen and for the true independence of France, which was the first victim of its own centralism. For there is a Basque people and a Breton people, but Jacobinism and industrialization have liquidated our people. Today there is nothing left but the French masses.

The Maoists in France

I am not a Maoist. I think that is why I was asked to write an introduction to these investigations. In most of them, the militants' testimony is objective but very much confined to their group. Since I am addressing a larger public here, perhaps it would be better to introduce the Maoists from the outside first, as they appear to their friends. I will describe the three characteristics which struck me when I became acquainted with several of them and which still strike me as I read over this collection of interviews.

One of their ideas is that a socialist must be violent, because he has a goal in mind which the ruling class rejects completely. Apparently this idea was adopted around 1950. Khrushchev came and laid the foundations for "peaceful coexistence," which amounted to endorsing revisionism. Then de Gaulle took power here and the leftist parties were crushed. No one talked about violence any more. The left lay low, waiting for an electoral victory to give them power in a peaceful way. In the sixties, one could not talk about the sound principle of revolutionary violence without being called an intellectual adventurist; 1958–1968 were years which can be spoken of only in very modest terms.

Introduction to Maos en France *by Michèle Manceaux, Éditions Galli-mard,* 1972.

And then violence broke out and raged over the whole area. Actually, neither the students nor the workers started it. In a somewhat confused way they announced certain major demands which the bourgeoisie did not want to listen to, and instantly they became the objects of police violence. In this way they came to know their own violence; they realized that the old bourgeois society was doomed and was only protecting itself from death with the clubs of policemen. Betrayed, the movement seemed to end. Not because of failure; there had never been any question of taking power *then*, except in the minds of a few politicians who did not fight.

When the violence seemed to be coming to an end, there were some groups who tried to keep it alive among themselves and to revive it among the masses. The Maoists were the first of these; from the beginning they adopted Mao Tsetung's slogan, "Political power grows out of the barrel of a gun." There were no guns, which means that in France the masses had not reached the stage of armed struggle. Even so the Maoists, who were very aware of the long march ahead of them, wanted first of all to reawaken revolutionary violence by effective, more or less symbolic, pinpoint actions—not to put it back to sleep the way the leftist parties and the unions had. They renewed an old tradition which for a decade had apparently been eclipsed. At first they were merely active, without asking for anything and without forming any theory for their action. They knew and accepted the inevitable consequence of this strategy: since they wanted to overthrow the bourgeoisie by force, they were sooner or later going to fall before the arsenal of bourgeois laws. That is what they first taught me, or rather retaught me: it was no longer the moment to sign petitions, or to make speeches in front of crowds at authorized meetings. (Since so many meetings are not allowed to take place, we must ask why this particular one which we are about to hold has been allowed by the authorities.) A revolutionary is committed to illegal action.

They went even farther. When they asked me to be editor of *La Cause du peuple* they were trying—and it will be seen that they clearly succeeded—to show that even though they took responsibility for their illegality, the government could not try to turn the repressive laws of the bourgeoisie against them without itself stepping outside the law, outside *its own* law. On the day of the trial of Le Dantec and Le Bris, former editors of the paper, Marcellin thought to make a bold move by dissolving the Gauche prolétarienne, an act of bravado which he accompanied by an awkwardly cynical speech. I am dissolving this political party, he said, because its militants will *necessarily* try to reorganize it and I will be able to throw them in prison. He was wrong. The Maoists had seen this coming long before and did not intend to put their little group back together, but rather to grow, to reach other sectors. They felt that the forms of action associated with the Gauche prolétarienne had fulfilled their function and that their time was over. What remained was *La Cause du peuple* which, Marcellin decided, was the organ of the Gauche prolétarienne. To publish it therefore amounted to resurrecting a faction that had been dissolved. During Le Dantec's trial, the public prosecutor—in other words the spokesman for the Minister of the Interior—demanded that the magistrate suspend publication of the newspaper for one year. It did not work; the magistrate, no doubt thinking he had already gone too far, refused.

Since it had not been banned, *La Cause du peuple* could continue to appear. Yet starting in June 1970, the government began seizing the issues at the printer's even though no judge was familiar with their contents and therefore could not legally order the seizure. The government had deliberately placed itself outside the law. As a matter of fact, in the fall of 1968 Geismar had intended to publish a journal in which "the masses would inform the masses" of oppression in various areas as well as of what actions had been taken, so that individuals who were carrying out their own struggles would never feel isolated for lack of information. The project came to nothing but was later taken up again under the name of *La Cause du peuple*. Thus the newspaper which was intended to be suppressed now belonged both to everyone and to no one in particular. For the most part the articles came from workers and country people, who described in their own writing or to interviewers their strikes, their acts of sabotage, their occupation of the lands of absentee landlords. They spoke not in the language of one party but in the language of the people, and the violence that came to light came from the people.

Tens of thousands of copies were saved from the police and sent all over France. Marcellin, who could not stop the newspaper from coming out and who was not willing to bring charges against its third editor (as he should have, according to the law) had the sellers and distributors arrested in Paris and in the country. Not trusting the "correctionelle" [Court of Summary Jurisdiction], he had them prosecuted before an emergency court, the Cour de Sûreté de L'État [State Security Court]. This body did everything he wanted it to do, even compounding most of the sentences with complete loss of civil rights. Young people found carrying only *two* copies of the same issue were sent to prison without the possibility of suspended sentences. During this time the "Friends of *La Cause du peuple*" distributed it with impunity in the streets of Paris.

After having fought for a long time, straining the law again and again, the government realized that since it represented the bourgeois law, it could not continue these illegal practices. One day it simply withdrew the policemen who had been laying siege to the printers for months, and all of a sudden we saw *La Cause du peuple* on the newsstands. Side by side with *France-Soir* and *l'Humanité*, it seemed just as illegal as it had in the preceding months when it had been banned. Its articles—brutal, unrefined, simplistic, but true —resounded with the voice of the people, and that is just what its bourgeois readers could not tolerate. They learned that the masses violently rejected slavery, in other words, the exploitative society in general. The bourgeois could not listen to this voice. They could put up with the revisionists talking to *them about* the masses, but not the masses talking *among themselves* without caring whether or not the bourgeois were listening. In the end, it had been proved that *La Cause du peuple* was *by its very nature* opposed to the legality of its capitalist society. Yet the government could not take the slightest step to make it an outlaw without becoming an outlaw itself. The Maoists had shown that the only relationship possible between the ruling class and the masses was a violent one.

Well, the revisionists will say, so the Maoists believe in the spontaneity of the masses, a myth which Lenin put an end to long ago. They really deserve the name given them— "Mao-Spontex." In the interview with Jean which you will read here, the true significance of this accusation is revealed. In 1968 Jean was an organizer at Contrexéville. Working conditions were horrifying; they called the factory "Buchenwald." But there had never been a strike in all the twelve years of its existence—this was the effect of terror. Atomizing forces acted constantly on the workers and serialized them. A group is said to be a serial group when each of its members, though he may be in the same circumstances as all the others, remains alone and defines himself according to his neighbor insofar as his neighbor thinks *like the others*. That is, each is something other than himself and behaves like someone else, who in turn is other than himself. The workers articulated and confirmed serial thinking as though it were their own thinking, but it was actually the thinking of the ruling class, who imposed it on the workers from the outside. Not that they found it either accurate or clear, but it justified their passivity by its reference to larger considerations. As Jean rightly says, if by some chance the I.F.O.P. or the S.O.F.R.E.S.* were to conduct a survey of the Contréxeville workers, it would find that many of the answers stemmed from serial ideology: racism ("You can't do anything with immigrant workers"), defiance toward the surrounding communities ("The Vosgiens are country people; they don't understand us"), sexual chauvinism ("Women are too stupid"), and so on. By its very principles, this type of survey has the effect of serializing, and it is being conducted elsewhere on subjects who are already serialized. In this sense Lenin is right. The mistake lies in believing that vital thought can be separated from action, that it is the specialty of "intellectuals," while action (without thought?) is the specialty of manual workers.

Actually, there is another, more profound thought which the ruling class represses by its atomization, and which is *the workers'* thought: it is the rejection of their condition. Exploited and oppressed in a basic way, they cannot become aware of this situation without revolting against it in the most radical fashion. But when the masses are atomized and serialized, when each person feels alone and partly resigned, this thought does not come to them in a recognizable form. It is masked by serial thought, which separates them and justifies the separation. Yet look at what happens as soon as an exterior change affects production, reveals the actual conditions at one point in the process, and provokes a particular, concrete, and precise refusal on the part of the workers. The series is then replaced by a group whose behavior expresses —though often without formulating it—the radical refusal to be exploited. At first, serial thinking opposes practical unity, in the same way that atomization and serialism oppose the formation of the group. It would be useless to refute such thinking with arguments, because it arises from the serial formation and expresses it perfectly. But as soon as

---

* Public opinion polls. I.F.O.P.: Institut Français d'Opinion Publique. S.O.F.R.E.S.: Societé Française d'Enquêtes par Sondage. [Translators' note.]

concrete action calls for unification—even if it is only temporary—serial thinking no longer has a place, because the group
can never think or act in a serial way. Jean shows clearly that
racism, sexism, and so forth, disappear the moment action
is taken. This happens not because the mechanisms have
been noticed, identified, and verbally denounced, but because they are facets of the separatist idea, which is no longer
needed. From that point on, as Jean says, the masses progress by leaps and bounds.

In the beginning at Contrexéville, when the workers
were completely encumbered and restrained by bourgeois
ideology, it would have been useless to suggest to them anything more than a symbolic, one-hour-long strike. But soon
the preparations for this strike brought about the beginnings
of the unification it required. Of their own accord the
masses transformed the symbolic work stoppage into a true
strike, an effective and open-ended strike which was inspired
by the real thinking of the group—the unconditional refusal
to be exploited. This decision, which surprised even Jean
himself, shows that when the masses begin to act, they inevitably go even farther than the agitators dare hope.

In a period of serialization, therefore, the first job for the
organizer is to support the most left-wing faction, even (or
most of all) if it is confused and timid, and to propose a
specific action, however modest. If the workers accept the
proposal, the second and most important duty of the organizer is to remain sensitive to their developing consciousness
and go along with them, not to try to lead them. What remains now is the question of their unity. There is no doubt
that after the strike, even if it is successful, the group is in
danger of falling back into seriality. This means that a *party of
the masses*, as the Maoists envisage it, should be constantly
sensitive to the group, should take its cue from the group and
keep attempting to bring the periods of seriality closer to the
periods of action. In some sense the party would become
primarily the memory of the masses. This is what the Mao-

ists call "spontaneity." It simply means that revolutionary thinking is born of the people and that the people alone can develop it fully through their acts. And of course, they are aware that in France there is no such thing yet as the People. For what is the People if not the masses as a whole freeing themselves by force from seriality? But wherever the masses reach the stage of *praxis* locally, they *are already* the People at the beginning of its realization.

That is the Maoists' second idea. Though the third is less explicit, it is no less important. It derives from the other two and you will find it on every page of this book. It is often—and in my opinion wrongly—called anti-authoritarianism. It goes without saying that the Maoists should be Marxist in the same sense as Guevara when he told me in 1959: "It is not our fault that the truth is Marxist." But one could do as Engels often did, particularly in *Anti-Dühring*, and in place of the history that men make, substitute an economy which is made by them but also without them, in a sense. For the Maoists, on the other hand, everywhere that revolutionary violence is born among the masses, it is immediately and profoundly moral. This is because the workers, who have up to that point been the objects of capitalist authoritarianism, become the subjects of their own history, even if only for a moment. The bourgeoisie, with all its "knowledge," never says more than "one thing: obey."* Many young people, fed up with working within plans established by the ruling bureaucracy, have joined the struggle of the masses because of its morality.

I know that the revisionists make morality out to be a superstructure of capitalist society. According to them the militant should not trouble himself about it; he should concentrate on practical rules and aim only at efficiency. And it is true that morality is the superstructure of the ruling class, but it is also true that this morality is a joke, since it is necessarily built upon exploitation. Yet even though the

---

* *Cahiers de la Gauche prolétarienne*, no. 2, May 1970, p. 69.

economic and political motives of the explosions of popular violence are obvious, the explosions cannot be explained except by the fact that these motives were *morally* appreciated by the masses. That is, the economic and political motives helped the masses to understand what is the highest immorality—the exploitation of man by man. So when the bourgeois claims that his conduct is guided by a "humanistic" morality—work, family, nation—he is only disguising his deep-seated immorality and trying to alienate the workers: he will never be moral. Whereas the workers and the country people, when they revolt, are completely moral because they are not exploiting anyone. That is the reason why the intellectual has nothing to teach them. Of course he has discovered exploitation and oppression, but only in an abstract way and as a simple contradiction of bourgeois morality. Only from the people, only by joining in a popular action, can he learn what it means to refuse to obey.

What the masses want *first of all*, if the Maoists are to be believed, is freedom. They are not refusing to work, but to do work that has been imposed on them—to work in rhythms, for example, that are established with profit in mind rather than the workers. It was this elementary demand for freedom which transformed the occupation of factories in 1936 and the lock-ins in 1967–1971 into *festivals*. A great deal was said about these lock-ins, and after some hesitation the organs of the left acknowledged that they constituted a form of spontaneous fighting invented by the masses and were therefore legitimate. Only the Maoists also recognized a specific affirmation of freedom of work. This affirmation shows that there is nothing idealistic about the aspiration toward freedom and that its source is always the concrete and material conditions of production. In each case, however, the material conditions do not prevent the workers from understanding that theirs is an attempt to put together a *moral* society—in other words, a society in which man, no longer alienated, will be able to find himself in his real relationship with the group.

Violence, spontaneity, morality: for the Maoists these are the three immediate characteristics of revolutionary action. The Maoists are not being overly simplistic; they do not say that theory is practice, but rather that theory never appears except in practice. This is the source of their agility in conceiving and carrying through local action which always originates among the masses. Theirs are struggles to force the establishment of a free revolutionary press and popular courts, struggles which are less and less symbolic and isolated and more and more realistic—like their fights against racism. Their struggles tend to be organized for the larger purpose of joining together to form the beginnings of a *politics* of the masses, a politics that must necessarily come into being. The classical leftist parties have remained in the nineteenth century, in the time of competitive capitalism. But though the Maoist movement is still in its first stages, these militants, with their anti-authoritarian *praxis*, appear to be the only revolutionary force capable of adapting to new forms of the class struggle in a period of organized capitalism.

Justice and the State

I have not been accused of any crime in Belgium. Yet I have never seen—and probably never will again—such a gathering of judges and lawyers. Because Justice must be impartial, the fact that the offenses with which I am charged and for which I assume responsibility took place in another country guarantees me an impartiality I would not find in France. Thus it is before you, gentlemen, that I will present my defense. It is not the same defense that I will be presenting in Paris to answer the accusation of libel that has been leveled against me; here I will attempt to take a more general point of view. I have entitled my lecture Justice and the State. This title might seem rather pretentious, since what is involved is only a misdemeanor stemming from journalistic activities. But it so happens that in France today, even the least significant trial raises the question of the fundamental relationship between Justice and the State. It was General de Gaulle who strongly emphasized this relationship. When he was asked to allow the Russell Tribunal to sit in France, he answered me in a published letter: "You will not be the one to teach me that all Justice, in principle as well as in practice, belongs only to the State."

Lecture delivered on February 25, 1972, at the invitation of the Jeune Barreau de Bruxelles (Young Lawyer's Association of Brussels).

I will therefore try to understand what justice in a bourgeois democracy—France—consists of, and I will attempt to apply the concepts that I formulate to my own case.

On one point history supports de Gaulle: since the late Middle Ages, the tribunal has been a correlative of the development of the state apparatus. In the beginning the Germanic peoples did not have organized judicial forms. For them, the *normal* judicial response to a case of damages was *compensation in kind*. At the time of feudalism, justice had become an obligatory service rendered primarily by the lords, and they drew the profits from it. In fact, a third of feudal revenues came from judicial revenues. That is to say, it was profitable because the plaintiffs had to pay for it. Between two men who sought to benefit from the law of *compensation*, a third would appear and say: "I am impartiality, I am justice. This is my decision, and you must submit to it"—which implied a kind of military power. Then came the king, who brought together the three independent powers of the treasury, the army, and justice. The parliament of the late thirteenth century, the royal army, and the great financial system perfected by Philippe le Bel were more or less contemporaneous.

During the Revolutionary disturbances of 1789–1794, when the bourgeoisie wanted to impose its power on the people, it created a new judicial system and replaced the great movements of the common people by specialized bodies such as the Revolutionary tribunal. These bodies were supposed to have originated among the people, but in fact they were created by the movement. Then the idea developed that the judges were neutral toward the two parties appearing before them, and that they judged impartially according to ideas and values which were labeled absolute but which were in fact a product of bourgeois ideology. Thus the judicial body was, and has remained up to the present, a bureaucracy appointed by the state and backed up by the state's "forces of order"—the police and, if need be, the army. Bourgeois justice seems, as de Gaulle said, to belong to the state both in principle and in practice.

However, I will make two objections to this theory. The first is based on the distinction between the state, which is an abstract reality, and the government, which is a concrete reality. Montesquieu—and then the revolutionary deputies who followed him after 1798—strongly emphasized that the impartiality of judges must be based on their independence from the government. "There can be no freedom when judicial power is not separated from legislative and executive power. If it were combined with legislative power, the power over the life and liberty of the citizens would be arbitrary, for the judge would be a legislator. If it were combined with executive power, the judge would have the force of an oppressor." This principle of the separation of the three powers is still advocated in our democracy. We must, then, try to understand what it means and decide whether or not the post-Gaullist Republic is still applying it.

The second objection, which is infinitely more important, is the notion that justice originates not in the state but among the people. For the people—that is, for the majority of Frenchmen—situations are basically either just or unjust. Ideology is not involved here, but a much deeper feeling which expresses the fundamental nature of the popular conscience. No social or political activity could have popular support if it were not felt to be just. On the other hand, the justice of a cause inspires enthusiasm and dedication, and induces certain groups to undertake actions which the official magistrates judge punishable according to a code that has been handed down to them and principles that have been instilled in them. As an example I need mention only the lock-ins of management or staff, which the bourgeoisie judges to be intolerable crimes and which aside from their political and social importance, have an important incentive: moral indignation and the desire for justice.

Stated in other terms, justice is rooted in the people.

When I say this, I mean that the oppressed and exploited can, under certain circumstances, demand their *liberation*, demand an end to oppression and exploitation. Michel Foucault, who sides with the Gauche prolétarienne, says that popular justice does not depend on any absolute principle: if a *damage* is done to it, it *demands compensation*. Today the damage, in this sense, is what we call the exploitation of man by man. The compensation at any particular stage will be a series of actions attempting here and now, in the present circumstances, to put an end to practices of exploitation. The Justice which "belongs to the State" obviously knows nothing about this compensation and would be incapable of understanding it, since State Justice was created precisely in order to perpetuate exploitation. To cite Foucault again, its role since the eighteenth century has been to set up two categories of the masses in opposition to each other. One category consists of the men who are forced to accept work at a very low salary and who are considered blameless: they accept a situation they cannot avoid. These are the members of the proletariat. The second category consists of those who reject the conditions of exploitation and who are therefore guilty of the misdemeanor of vagrancy. But it must be noted that the first *resign themselves* to agreeing to the so-called work contract which buys their work force at a low price. Often they find liberty—or the will to be liberated—deep within themselves and end up rebelling, thus becoming subject to the same penalties that are applied to vagrants.

So there exist in France two kinds of justice. One is bureaucratic justice, which ties the proletariat to its condition. The other is primitive justice, which is the profound movement of the proletariat and the common people asserting their freedom against proletariatization. When de Gaulle declares that all Justice belongs to the State, he is either mistaken or showing his true character, for the source of all justice is the people. The government takes advantage of the tendency toward justice that it finds in the common people and creates organs of justice that represent the bureaucratization of the people's will to justice. These courts pass judgment by simply applying the law, and they draw their inspiration from bourgeois principles. Thus they are based on fraud and a falsification of the popular will. In choosing between the two kinds of justice, the one codified and permanent, the other irregular and primitive, you must therefore be aware that they are contradictory. If you choose one, you will be held accountable by the other.

I have chosen popular justice as the deeper form of justice, the only true justice. Which leaves me open to attack by bourgeois justice. I made this choice after May 1968, and it was the only one that I could make. May 1968 began as a revolt of the students against bourgeois culture; then a little later it turned into the greatest wave of strikes that France has ever known.

What does this revolt against bourgeois culture mean?

Bourgeois culture is a totality. Those whom the sociologists Bourdieu and Passeron call the "inheritors"—that is, the bourgeois sons of bourgeois fathers—are immersed from childhood in this culture and do not have much trouble assimilating it completely during the course of their education. Bourgeois culture claims to be humanistic. So far, however, it has profited by the error of the bourgeoisie—which considered itself to be the "universalist class" during the Revolution—and confuses humanity with the bourgeoisie, refusing to consider the proletarians as whole men simply because they are not bourgeois. This is what allows it to create the type of teaching we call *elitist*, which starts in early childhood. Based on selection and competition, it eliminates more and more students and ends by forming a kind of elite of finalists which serves as a base for the complex hierarchies of the bourgeois system.

The elite has been filled with a knowledge that is supposed to be universal, while in reality it is only the minimum required by businesses in order to hire these young people.

If they attain the position of finalists in the championship, this knowledge then becomes abstract: it is separated from the things on which it was established. At the same time, it becomes a kind of *power*, that is, the capacity to call upon other men and impose tasks on them. Moreover, the university is a place for empty talk: there, *nothing* is taught to *few people*. The students, especially those from *petit bourgeois* backgrounds and those who are sons of workers, understand that many are called and few are chosen, particularly in the social sciences. They know that bourgeois culture allows a great many individuals to enter its culture but rejects the majority and thus tends to create a proletariat of degree holders. It reserves for its elect the positions of testers and supervisors in businesses, where they can use the knowledge they have acquired to put the workers and staff to the test, or can use the principles of "human engineering" to deceive or pacify the workers. The elite do either no work or a kind of police work that will reinforce the hierarchy. But in May 1968 the students rejected both possibilities; that was one of the causes of what happened.

However, the workers went on strike too. Bourgeois culture did not suit them at all. It had established a hierarchy of bosses, and the workers found themselves at the very bottom, forced to obey and never allowed to lead. Because of this they saw the elite as they really are; that is to say, they looked up from the bottom at statues on pedestals which were crushing them. The statues were blind to the fact, though the workers could see it clearly enough. The workers perceived that bourgeois culture is a superstructure which tends to justify oppression and repression in the eyes of the bourgeoisie.

In a certain way, however, the bourgeois culture joins in the effort of massification in order to make sure that the proletariat will be impotent. It is absorbed by the workers and occasionally by the peasants as a negative divisive power. In fact, if the I.F.O.P. had decided to conduct polls among

workers in many of the businesses that had not had a strike
for five or ten years, it would certainly have received many
answers based on an ideology that included racism ("Nothing can be done about immigrant workers"), defiance toward
the surrounding communities ("The country people are too
stupid; they wouldn't help us"), sexism ("You can't get
anything from women"), and so on.

However, there is another, deeper kind of thinking among
the workers, which the ruling class suppresses in favor of its
ideology. This thinking is truly *their own*: it is the refusal
to accept their condition. The oppressed and exploited work
like convicts, with supervisors and foremen on their backs.
They cannot become conscious of this situation except by
rebelling against it in the most radical way. But when the
masses are atomized, when each person feels himself to be
alone and to some degree resigned to his impotence, the
deeper thinking does not occur to them in a very clear form.
It is disguised by bourgeois ideology, which separates them
and justifies their separation. In 1968, however, a change
of circumstances brought about a concrete and specific refusal on the part of the workers. Solitary individuals merged
into a group whose behavior expressed a radical rejection of
exploitation. Racism, sexism, and defiance toward the country people disappeared, not because these components of
bourgeois ideology had been identified and denounced, but
because they were facets of the separatist idea and were no
longer needed.

In brief, we can say that every popular movement, rejecting as it does the so-called bourgeois liberalism, is an active
affirmation of freedom. There are thus two types of culture
and two types of justice. The bourgeois culture, which is complex and diverse, is still founded on the oppression-repression
and exploitation that it requires. The popular culture, unrefined, violent, and hardly differentiated, is nevertheless the
only valid one, for it is based on the demand for absolute
freedom. And freedom should be understood to mean not

license but rather sovereignty and responsibility for each worker.

Simply by asserting the need to choose between these two cultures and two kinds of justice, one is already choosing the second. What stops many people from doing so is that they do not have to take any action in order to choose the first. Bourgeois culture and justice already hold their negative sway over large areas of the population. To choose popular culture and justice, on the other hand, one must opt for action at all times. This is because in France the people have been atomized; as an entity they no longer exist—or do not yet exist. But everywhere that the class struggle intensifies, the masses recover their unity and are therefore already the People at the beginning of its re-establishment. Then and only then do they rediscover deep within themselves their need for freedom and sovereignty, a need which underlies all popular needs. Anyone who chooses the People must therefore help to re-establish this concrete unity wherever he can. He will find himself involved in all forms of action demanding that the need for freedom and sovereignty be fulfilled.

For this reason, if an intellectual chooses the People, he must know that the time for signing manifestos, for quiet protest meetings, and for publishing articles in "reformist" newspapers is over. His task is not so much to speak as to try, by any means available to him, to *let the people speak for themselves*. It is from this point of view that the affair of *La Cause du peuple* must be understood.

In late 1968 or early 1969 Geismar described a certain project to me: he wanted to create a journal in which the masses would speak to the masses or, even better, in which the People, when it had been partially re-established through its struggles, would speak to the masses in order to bring them into the process of restoration. This meant that the journal would attempt to give an account of all the actions of the workers and country people in France. Thus if the workers who read it found themselves in a situation in which they were ready to engage in an active struggle, they would no longer feel isolated and would perhaps be inspired by descriptions of certain types of action—for example, the lock-ins, which might have been impossible in some places but possible in others. The project was just getting started and I was supposed to work on it with Geismar. Then, for practical reasons, he suddenly abandoned the idea. At that moment Geismar was not yet connected with the Gauche prolétarienne. He soon entered it, and the Maoists started a newspaper, *La Cause du Peuple*, which actually was the realization of our original project. As a matter of fact, the newspaper did not have an owner; it belonged to the People. It was sold in a militant fashion and included articles written directly or indirectly (in interview form) by workers. For the benefit of other workers, they gave accounts of action they had just taken or were then taking, or they described situations in various factories—that is, management practices creating tension among the workers, such as layoffs, lockouts, and increases in production quotas. The newspaper wanted to present the larger picture of struggles in France from 1970 on, using the words of the workers themselves. It created a scandal.

Why? Because the bourgeoisie is elitist. It assumes that the masses delegate their powers to an elite—a political elite, a journalistic elite. It can tolerate hearing qualified editors speak *of* the masses, or if absolutely necessary, *for* the masses. But these editors must speak in a *bourgeois language* with the type of reasoning sanctioned by the bourgeoisie. *L'Humanité* is no exception to this rule. In some leftist newspapers the editors have *come from* the People. But that is precisely the point: they have come away from it. Occasionally they register protests in the name of the People, but their tone is moderate and by this very fact they show that they have been co-opted. They are revisionists, even when they don't want to be. For even if they become advocates of the masses, they do not feel or no longer feel within themselves the lassitude, the anger, and the needs of the men for whom they are speaking. They can speak *about* these needs, but they turn them into statistical objects, quantities that can be foreseen as decreasing at a reasonable rate, that is, at a rate compatible with profit.

In *La Cause de peuple*, the complete reverse is true: the needs are expressed just as the workers feel them. The workers expose their indignation and even their hatred as oppressed people, emotions which are often intensified by defeat or victory. Their rough, primitive, and violent language deeply shocks the bourgeois. In the first place, none of the accepted forms are there. Take an article in *Le Monde*, in which the facts are put in the conditional to deprive them of all that might be disturbing, and in which the conclusion is always formed as a question. Compare it with an interview of a worker who talks about his fight against the bosses and which reads like war reporting. Read the slogans, which *La Cause de peuple* does not make up but simply prints ("Bercot, you bastard, the people will have your skin"), and you will see the difference. Here, the people speak to the people. This experience benefits the workers who are still atomized. A worker explains a particular fact that he knows well—for example, that the vast majority of work accidents are neither due to inattention on the part of the workers nor destined to happen from the beginning, but are outright murders. What he says, in short, is not addressed to the bourgeois reader, of whom nothing is expected and who does not feel any kinship with the message. It is the popular language that accompanies a certain stage in the struggle— exactly the kind of language the bourgeoisie does not want to recognize, because it ignores bourgeois subtleties and consistently affirms the popular morality and the popular meaning of justice. This is the very justice that has been stolen from the People and disfigured.

Language, I suppose, is the difference between the journal planned by Geismar and *La Cause du peuple*. It was inevitable. It should have been predictable that if the workers were allowed to speak, they would reveal, even in the very nature of their idiom, the profound rebellion of the exploited and the oppressed, that rebellion which the bourgeoisie would prefer to ignore.

All the more because the Assembly elected in 1968 was a "Nonesuch Chamber," as was said under the Restoration, and one which was brought to power by the rich elite's great fear. From the time it first convened, it claimed that May 1968 was over, that all trace of it had disappeared. As a result there was a blind and harsh wave of repression that weakened the student movement. But the workers remained combative: the number of lock-ins after 1968 increased considerably. What the Assembly wanted to hide, *La Cause du peuple* shouted from the rooftops. (Now and then it had a somewhat overtriumphant tone, but this fault gradually diminished.) As a consequence, the government arranged for a "coup" against *La Cause du peuple*. Its principal editor, Le Dantec, was arrested, as was a second editor, Le Bris. Then came the day of judgment. In order to influence the judges, the government announced that the Gauche prolétarienne was to be dissolved by an official measure. And in his indictment the prosecutor—who is entirely dependent on the executive branch—demanded that the judge punish the defendants severely and that he suspend *La Cause du peuple* for one year.

The result was not all that had been hoped for, perhaps because of the modicum of independence which judges had at that time. The defendants were harshly sentenced, but the judge refused to ban *La Cause du peuple*. The reason he gave was that no one owned it. That was correct, because it belonged to the People. But a more important reason for the magistrate's attitude seemed to be that although he would readily punish two men who were responsible for what he thought to be excesses of language, he felt that the suppression, however temporary, of the publication in which these excesses had appeared would be an attack on the freedom of the press.

Shortly before this sentence was passed, Geismar and his comrades had come to see me. Le Dantec and Le Bris were going to be convicted; another editor would have to be found. They suggested that I take the job, and I agreed. Here I must explain why.

I should first point out that if I accepted this proposal, it would necessarily change their political line. Until then *La Cause du peuple* had been hostile to intellectuals, to those who were called the "leading lights," and occasionally to me as well (for example, in several of its articles during the trial of Roland Castro). But they were at an impasse: if the new editor were not a well-known figure (and therefore a "leading light"), he would run the risk of being put in prison as soon as he took over his duties. They wanted to continue publishing *La Cause du peuple* openly as long as possible. Even though the manner in which the newspaper was sold was often rather militant, the time had not yet come to think of going underground. There was only one possibility: to approach a well-known intellectual.

But this solution would eventually induce the Maoists to think about the status of intellectuals and about the possibilities of undertaking joint action with them. It seemed to me that to broaden the idea of the People, to allow intellectuals to participate in their struggles, would be particularly beneficial. First of all, because I was an intellectual and was sympathetic to their cause. Secondly, because I was in favor of uniting the forces of the true left—and by this I mean something completely different from the partnership of the Socialist and Communist Parties. Now, if it was possible to bring the workers and intellectuals together in at least one area, there could be hope of eventually rebuilding the alliance of the intelligentsia and the proletariat which had been widespread in the nineteenth century and which the Communist Party had broken up. I will quickly add that I was not wrong. At the end of last year, workers and certain intellectuals came together in Dunkirk on the occasion of the Liscia affair. Many other cases could be cited. But this alliance called for some changes on both sides: On the one hand, certain prejudices of the former Gauche prolétarienne would have to disappear. On the other hand, the men who had only very recently been called "classical" intellectuals would have to protest as intellectuals against bourgeois repression, thereby changing their relationship to society.

But my most important motive was to save *La Cause du peuple,* the only newspaper which allowed the voice of the people to be heard. I should admit that I agreed to take the post because I was a well-known figure. Cynically, I took advantage of my fame; for the first time in my life I actually behaved like a "leading light." Why? To provoke a crisis within the repressive bourgeoisie.

The bourgeois have always been wary of intellectuals, and with reason. But they mistrust intellectuals because they see them as strange creatures who have emerged from their very midst. Most intellectuals were born of bourgeois parents who inculcated them with the bourgeois culture. They seem to be the guardians and the transmitters of this culture. In fact, a certain number of technicians of practical knowledge do eventually appoint themselves watchdogs of the culture, as Nizan called them. The others, having come out on top, remain elitist even when they profess revolutionary ideas. They are allowed to protest because they speak the bourgeois language, but they are subtly manipulated until the right moment comes, and then a chair in the Académie Française or a Nobel Prize or some other lure is enough to co-opt them. This is how it happens that a Communist writer is currently displaying his wife's memoirs at the Bibliothèque Nationale, in an exhibition that was inaugurated by the Minister of Education.*

* The reference is to Louis Aragon. [Translators' note.]

However, there are some intellectuals—and I am one—
who have no longer been willing to engage in dialogue with
the bourgeoisie since 1968. Actually, it is not that simple:
every intellectual has what can be called his ideological interests. For a writer, this means the totality of his work so
far. Even though I have always protested against the bourgeoisie, my works are addressed to it, are written in its language, and contain elitist elements—or at least the earliest
ones did. For the last seventeen years I have been engaged
in a work on Flaubert which can be of no interest to the
workers, since it is written in a complicated and definitely
bourgeois style. Furthermore, the first two volumes of this
work were bought and read by bourgeois reformists, professors, students, and the like. It was not written by the people
or for the people; it was the product of a bourgeois philosopher's reflections over the course of most of his life. Two
volumes have appeared, the third is at the printer, and I am
preparing the fourth. I am committed to it—meaning that
I am sixty-seven years old, I have been working on it since
I was fifty, and before that I dreamed about it.

Now, we must say that this work, assuming that it has
some value, by its very nature represents the age-old bourgeois swindle of the people. The book ties me to bourgeois
readers. Through it, I am still bourgeois and will remain so
as long as I continue to work on it. However, another side
of myself, which rejects my ideological interests, is fighting
against my identity as a classic intellectual. That side of me
knows very well that if I have not been co-opted, I have come
within a hair of it. And since I am challenging myself, since
I refuse to be an elitist writer who takes himself seriously, I
find myself among those who are struggling against the bourgeois dictatorship. I want to reject my bourgeois situation.
There is thus a very special contradiction within me: I am
still writing books for the bourgeoisie, yet I feel solidarity
with the workers who want to overthrow it. Those workers
were the ones who frightened the bourgeoisie in 1968 and

who are the victims of greater repression today. As one of them, I should be punished. Yet as the author of *Flaubert*, I am the *enfant terrible* of the bourgeoisie and should be co-opted.

It is therefore a question of communicating to the government the profound contradiction that lies within me. I am writing a work of literary history, and I have assumed editorship of *La Cause du peuple* and three other "leftist" newspapers, two of which have disappeared for financial reasons (*Tout* and *La Parole au peuple*) and have been replaced by a new bimonthly, *Revolution*, which I also direct. What does it mean to "direct"? First of all, I must admit that it is a challenge to the government. In effect I am saying: "You have sentenced Le Dantec to one year in prison and Le Bris to eight months. I am the third director; therefore arrest me. If you arrest me, you will have a political trial on your hands; if you do not arrest me, you will be showing that Justice has two different standards."

During Le Dantec's trial I went to the bench and expressed to the magistrate my amazement at being free while my two colleagues were behind bars. He told me that he couldn't do anything about it, and he was right: he could only judge the defendants who were brought before him. But in its indecision the government was making a fool of itself. It had been caught in the contradiction of my situation. There were those in the government who wanted to indict me. There were others who took their cue from what de Gaulle had said during the trial of the 121, feeling that a political trial could only do them harm and preferring to let it pass—just as, in fact, the bourgeois newspapers had originally advised them to do.

In the beginning the government was so embarrassed that it did not interfere with my first issue of *La Cause du peuple*, which appeared on May 1, 1970. Then for a period of many months the Minister of the Interior employed a new tactic: he no longer talked about the editor responsible for *La Cause du peuple*, but instead had each issue of the newspaper seized as soon as it came off the press. This tactic was absolutely illegal, since the judge had refused to ban the paper. Of course, individual articles might have been liable to prosecution. But no one could know that, because no one had read the newspaper before it was seized. It was thus not in application of the law of 1881, or the modifications of 1892, called the *lois scélérates* [outrageous laws], that the seizure was made. It was purely and simply a matter of smothering an organ of the revolutionary press by force.

The crime against the freedom of the press was obvious. Furthermore, the tactic was ineffective: we managed to distribute the great majority of copies, and the police were able to seize only what was left over. The Minister of the Interior then tried to take action against the people who were selling the newspaper. He arrested them everywhere he could and had them brought before an emergency court [*cour d'exception*] for having re-established the outlawed party. We proved once again that there were two standards of justice, because well-known intellectuals and I myself openly sold *La Cause du peuple* in the heart of Paris and were not interfered with. At the time of the first sale, a policeman took me by the arm and told me to follow him to the police station. I still remember his shock when someone in the crowd shouted out to him: "You're arresting a Nobel Prize!" He immediately let me go and rushed away. A group called Friends of *La Cause du peuple* was formed to give us support. All in all, the government tactic had failed—a fact which they themselves admitted after several attempts at seizure, so that one day the police simply stopped harassing the printer. *La Cause du peuple* was then freely sold on the newspaper stands—with the same contents that seem so scandalous compared with *France-Soir* or *L'Humanité*.

This was no solution, however: the right wing of the majority was understandably aware of the fact that I was escaping justice while Le Dantec and Le Bris had been found

guilty. Furthermore, a newspaper called *Minute* which belonged to the right-wing opposition was crying out for my
imprisonment. Again the government confined itself to a
half-hearted measure: it indicted me for libel. The plaintiffs
were the Keeper of the Seals, the Minister of Justice, and the
Minister of Interior. The incriminating articles had been
chosen from issues of *La Cause du peuple* and *Tout* dating
back to 1970, which means that according to French law
the charges were no longer valid. The prosecutor must have
taken official steps to obtain permission to ignore the statute
of limitations. I was indicted in June 1971. Charged and
freed on my own recognizance, I spent my vacation in Italy
as I do each year and came back in October for the prelim-
inary hearing, which was over very quickly. I was charged on
five counts. *When* will I be judged, and *how?*

When, I do not know. But to find out *how*, it would be
helpful to examine the history of the judiciary during these
post-Gaullist years.

There is no question that up to the time of the Fifth Republic, the independence of justice as Montesquieu described
it was a greater source of pride to the judges than any other
characteristic of the system. They refused to serve the government, whatever its political leanings, and during the years of
the Third and Fourth Republics they often asserted their
autonomy. In the 1950s the president of the Chambre des
mises en accusation [Grand Jury] freed Jacques Duclos, a
deputy whom the government claimed to have arrested in
the act of participating in a demonstration against General
Ridgway.

However, there is a general trait which does not belong
only to the present period—and I am pointing it out in order
to show the limits of judicial independence. The judge is almost always a bourgeois and the son of a bourgeois; his elitist
education thus began in childhood. He was put through a
competitive course of study, won certain prizes, and emerged
a product of this system, a member of the elite by virtue of his

ideology, his character, and his profession. Montesquieu wanted accused persons to be judged by their equals in the true sense of the word. This is clearly impossible: because he is the product of a competitive system based on the bourgeois idea that the finest things are the rarest things, the judge feels that he merits his power by his very rarity. He is an important member of the bourgeois hierarchy, and the defendants he judges seem to him to be his inferiors.

Foucault remarks that the topographical analysis of a courtroom—including the bench which separates the judge from the accused person and the witnesses, and the difference in levels between the judge and the others—is enough to indicate that the judge belongs to another species. No matters how impartial he might be, he will treat those who who come before him as objects and will make no attempt to understand the subjective motives of their acts as these would appear to the defendants. In any case he is remote from popular justice, which rarely appears in a court and which has a completely different topography. Figuratively speaking, the witnesses and experts in a court of popular justice file past in the highest place and the judges are down in the main part of the room, the jury being the public. But these remarks have little to do with the present period. They merely attempt to show what kind of impartiality I expect from a judge. Let us say that I expect class impartiality, which is a natural wish, since I am going to be appearing before the justice of the bourgeoisie.

What we see in our own period, on the other hand, is a tendency on the part of the Gaullist bourgeoisie to limit the independence of bourgeois justice. It would like not only a class justice, but a party justice. De Gaulle's remark about justice, which I quoted before, is interpreted by the present government to mean that the judicial branch should take orders from the executive branch. Actually, the government today thinks that it has a twofold mission: it wants both to give France up to private enterprise, and to integrate the working class into bourgeois society, not by improving the condition of the proletariat but by the constant use of repression. It keeps bourgeois ideology and the code of the nineteenth century as a cover, but it knows very well that both are out of date. It represses by distorting the present laws or by having new ones passed. In either case a judge who must apply these laws can no longer identify with them.

As an example of distorted laws, take the Geismar affair. A meeting was held to protest the arrest of Le Bris and Le Dantec, and the five thousand or so present were shouting, "On the twenty-seventh, we take to the streets!" Several speakers who shared their feelings spoke before this crowd of overexcited people. Only one of the speakers was arrested —Geismar, who spoke for eight minutes and said nothing more extreme than any of the others. He *alone* is held responsible for what took place on the twenty-seventh. What actually did happen? No one will say. No medical certificates were brought forward; there was no testimony to support the case of the prosecution. The prosecution admitted, in fact, that it was a question of "contusions and not serious injuries." What was more, it was established that the police were the ones who started the disturbance at Censier by throwing tear-gas grenades. The demonstrators responded by throwing back the pins. On the other side, at the quay, the police did not fire and the demonstrators, not having been provoked, did not counterattack. It is clear that the decision to demonstrate crystallized at the meeting and that the forces of order wanted to strike back harshly, even violently. Unfortunately, no policemen were wounded. It didn't matter; Geismar was guilty in advance; he was sentenced to eighteen months, with no parole. It was because he was one of the leaders of the Gauche prolétarienne, about which Marcellin had said on the radio: "I am dissolving this party because its members will want to re-establish it and then we will be able to put them in prison." As we can see, a former member of the Gauche prolétarienne is guilty in advance. That is what happened to Geismar: the bourgeois guarantees had been denied to him; there was no need to prove his guilt; it had been established a priori. He had been found guilty according to pre-existing laws, but laws that had been grossly tampered with.

The affair of the Friends of *La Cause du peuple* shows how one first tampers with the law, then goes on to pass a new, unconstitutional law because the earlier one was insufficient. The Friends declared itself an association to the Prefecture of Police, which was supposed to give it authorization. This is the law: every new organization announces its existence and is *recognized*, even if it should later be harassed and dissolved. For the first time in France since the law was enacted, the Prefect of Police, following the instructions of Marcellin, refused to give us authorization. The government was not concerned with either harassing or accepting our association, but preferred to reject it *against the law*. We brought suit and the court ruled in our favor: a good example of independence. We were therefore granted authorization.

But the government, which was now very displeased, had its docile majority quickly push through a new law making it possible to refuse authorization when this was judged necessary. Under the new edict the court was ultimately responsible for whether or not authorization should be given. We can see that the law not only severely compromised the freedom of assembly, but also attempted to make the judge the accomplice of a particular politics. Only politics, in fact, can furnish the motivation for rejecting or accepting an organization, since criminal organizations, when they exist, are clandestine. Fortunately, the constitutional council showed discretion and rejected the law as unconstitutional. What is significant in this episode is the sequence of events: the government tampers with one law and then proceeds to vote in an unconstitutional law, in other words, an illegal law. In this particular case, justice was well defended. Can as much be said when it is a question of applying new, regularly voted in and unconstitutional laws such as the anti-vanda!ism and antidrug laws? The judge must apply them because they have been approved by vote. But no one knows what he really thinks of them; it can easily happen that he enforces the law even though he is opposed to it. What becomes of his independence when the judgment he gives contradicts his ideology or the will of the people which is expressed in the code?

Yet we must not stop here. The fact is that judges are given cases to decide which they are not allowed to know very much about. In point of fact my case, like those of so many French people—especially the young—since 1968 is political in nature. Now, there is no such thing as a political crime in France. If there were, one would have to recognize that *another* politics exists (one which has to be ignored), and the mere fact of practicing it would be enough to have you taken to court. In fact this politics does exist; it is *revolutionary* socialism. It used to be Communism, but since that large party has become part of the respectable opposition, there remains only one kind of politics which is forbidden: the politics that aims to overthrow the bourgeoisie through violence. Even to state this fact would be to publicize the forbidden politics. Thus we can see how judges with very little independence—unfortunately, they do exist in France—are obliged in court to separate the violence from the politics behind it. They must cut it off from its goals and its purpose and turn it into a common-law misdemeanor.

Among other examples I remember the trial of the militant Roland Castro, in which I was a witness and which I followed from beginning to end. Castro—an activist of the V.L.R., which has since disbanded on its own decision—had joined his comrades and some intellectuals in occupying the office of the C.N.P.F. [Conféderation National du Patronat Français]. They were protesting the death of five immigrant workers who had been asphyxiated by gas when they had tried to use it as a source of heat. This symbolic and peaceful occupation, in which Maurice Clavel, Michel Leiris, and Jean Genet also participated, was an attempt to point out to the public the people who were truly responsible for these deaths—the French bosses. The C.R.S. [Compagnie Républicaine de Securité, or riot police] was called to the offices of the C.N.P.F. and violently removed the protestors, who did not offer the slightest resistance. The police struck all of them, and pushed Maurice Clavel and Jean Genet down a staircase. They brutally forced the protestors whom they could catch into police wagons and hauled them to the station. All were soon released except Roland Castro, who had left the police wagon at a red light and tried to escape. He was caught, held and struck, and at the station he was charged with assaulting an officer. Still, it had to be proved. When the two policemen had caught him, they had gripped him tightly, twisting his arm and so on, and it was difficult to see how his reactions could have constituted an assault against the officers. They therefore had to testify, in spite of seventeen witnesses to the contrary, that they had caught him a first time, that he had violently broken free and run away, and that they had run after him and caught him again.

But what counts here is the offense. Castro, outraged by the manner in which French management treated immigrants, unlawfully occupied premises that were not his property. This is what an elitist judge who respected property could reproach him for. Castro's defense was political: he had exposed and passed judgment on management policy toward the immigrants. There was no question of such defense being taken seriously for even one moment, though most of the defense witnesses and lawyers eagerly attempted to present it. The problem became very simple. Had there been, or had there not been, officers outside, in front of the door of the wagon, and had Castro pushed them as he was getting out? This militant could just as well have been a thief or a drunkard arrested for disturbing the peace. Not one word was said about the police brutality at the C.N.P.F. office, which easily could have justified his attempt at escape. And yet we are asked to tell the *whole* truth.

But the judge wanted the whole truth concerning an infinitesimal incident: were these two men in such and such a place? And none of us could understand why the event was not dealt with in its totality—that is, by starting with government and management policies. To tell the *whole* truth about an infinitesimal instant is a pure contradiction. Truth develops over time. In a closed, limited instant, there can be no truth. But if the truth had been established, if the discussion had included the deaths of the black workers and the occupation of the C.N.P.F., the trial would have been political. This was something which neither the government (and its representative, the prosecutor) nor the judge wanted. From that point on, the outcome was obvious: Castro was found guilty. The scandal came to an end when the militants in the prisons went on a hunger strike to demand political status. It was given to them, under a false name.

There is an even more serious aspect to contemporary state justice: judges have been turned into abstractions. They give their verdict and sentence the defendant to a prison term—but without realizing it, they have levied a much heavier penalty. In their eyes and in the eyes of the law, the sentence is simply the deprivation of freedom. But for the past ten years there has been a steady deterioration in French prisons. Guards beat the prisoners, and an internal court—often directed by a single person—sentences them for a mere trifle to the *mitard*, an unheated cell in which they remain half naked for one or two weeks. When a prisoner attempts suicide, which often happens, he is put in a straitjacket for several days, forced to defecate in place, and left to wallow in his excrement for long periods. The guards watch the prisoners, the guards watch the guards, and some prisoners even watch the guards. The penal administration rules supreme, which means that the sentences are carried out by this headless body, this group of poorly paid functionaries who are recruited without screening, who are afraid of the prisoners, and who little by little become sadists. When the judge sentences the defendant to a year's loss of freedom, he has in fact sentenced him to much worse. He has put the prisoner into the hands of an administration which has total control over him. This deterioration in prisons is partly intentional, for the Keeper of the Seals is carrying out the policy of the government, constantly striking down the people on the fringe of society and the young. A question that interests me personally is what the judge thinks when he gives his sentence. Is he really abstract, as I have said, and unaware of the truth, or has he allowed himself to be won over by the politics of the regime?

In fact—and this is the last point I will discuss—judges are subjected to considerable pressures. First, there are what I will call external pressures—and I am not even speaking of the concern of the magistrates for their own advancement. I am referring to the kind of pressure that was applied, for example, when the judiciary as a whole was insulted by an important deputy from the majority, Tomasini, who reproached it for cowardice because he felt that it did not come through with enough convictions. Furthermore, it is not safe for a judge to tell the truth. The sentencing judge [*le juge d'application des peines*] at Toul was deaf as a doornail, which is symbolic. But the judge at Clairvaux had his eyes and ears open. He made a long report to the Keeper of the Seals on the Clairvaux prison and was immediately replaced, which proves that when Pleven must choose between a judge and the penal administration, he automatically chooses the administration. One will understand this when one learns that before the revolt, the director of the prison at Toul was held to be the best administrator of the period. Imagine how great the pressures will be in my case, since one of the two plaintiffs is the Minister of Justice.

Then there are also pressures which I will call *internal*,

that is, pressures inherent to the judicial system. The judge needs the police, who belong to the Minister of the Interior. He must treat them with consideration, and it is rare that he convicts a policeman of anything. Policemen are sworn in, and when they testify, they are unconditionally taken at their word. In Castro's case, two policemen maintained that they were in front of the police wagon door, seventeen witnesses contradicted their statement, but it was the policemen who were believed. This is particularly serious today, because the French police have changed a great deal since the Algerian war. They often use violence without cause; there are fascists, racists, and former members of the O.A.S. among them. Now, if it happens that these policemen are too rough with someone, they often claim that the person —no matter what his size and strength—has assaulted them. The judge believes them as a matter of course, for he cannot do otherwise. The system thus forces him to protect men who are often no more than bullies and sadists, if not murderers.

Justice is therefore compelled to apply laws that have been tampered with or new laws that are unconstitutional. It does not have the means to judge a political offense and must necessarily reduce it to an offense of common law. This was seen recently in the trial of the newspaper *Coupure*, which had reprinted the articles from *La Cause du peuple* which the prosecutor had cracked down on during Le Dantec's trial. The president of the court said to a witness: "We do not engage in politics here." If politics are not engaged in, then what the devil were they talking about? The government considers Justice to be under its orders and subjects it to violent pressures. Justice must be considerate to the police and believe the testimony of policemen. The sentences that Justice pronounces are not the ones that the sentenced man undergoes. Am I saying that the government has succeeded in taking the judiciary's bourgeois independence away from it? Not yet, but the situation has become worse, and one must admire the judges who resist and who are still independent. All the more so because most of the time their background and culture are bourgeois, and they can hardly be said to share the views of the revolutionaries who come before them. They have nothing to sustain them other than the abstract idea of independence.

This is the situation of my judges concerning political offenses and, as a consequence, the offense I am accused of. I do not know who my judges will be. Until now I have had dealings only with three examining magistrates. They all behaved correctly, but only one gave me his hand when I entered his office. Was it a mild attack of conscience? At a party or reception the others would certainly have shaken my hand. The most I can hope for from the magistrates who will be convicting me is that they will conscientiously do their job, which is to apply the laws of class justice. The worst would be for me to be assigned to one of the judges who have given up their independence. In that case I would be judged indirectly by Pleven and Marcellin, those important plaintiffs who scarcely feel any affection for me.

There is not the slightest doubt that I have been eager to help liberate popular ethics and justice: this is my crime. A popular court would acquit me. But how can I reasonably think that a member of society's elite would be able to lower himself—if it can be called lowering himself—to the level of the oppressed and exploited people and to consider *with the eyes of the people* the crushing pedestals on which the bourgeois hierarchy sits? Nothing allows me to hope for that. I do not think I will be sentenced to prison. Or if I am, perhaps the sentence will be suspended. But I imagine—for this is the usual government practice—that a heavy fine will be imposed on me to cure me of my desire to leave my class. That is the price I will pay for having used my trial as a platform and having presented a political defense of a crime that cannot be political, since the government does not believe that such a thing exists.

Elections: A Trap
for Fools

In 1789 the vote was given to landowners. What this meant
was that the vote had been given not to men but to their
real estate, to bourgeois property, which could only vote for
itself. Although the system was profoundly unfair, since it
excluded the greater part of the French population, it was
not absurd. The voters, of course, voted individually and in
secret. This was in order to separate them from one another
and allow only incidental connections between their votes.
But all the voters were property owners and thus already isolated by their land, which closed around them and with its
physical impenetrability kept out everything, including people. The ballots were discrete quantities that reflected only
the separation of the voters. It was hoped that when the votes
were counted, they would reveal the common interest of the
greatest number, that is, their class interest. At about the
same time, the Constituent Assembly adopted the Le Chapelier law, whose ostensible purpose was to put an end to the
guilds but which was also meant to prohibit any association
of workers against their employers. Thus passive citizens
without property, who had no access to indirect democracy
(in other words, to the vote which the rich were using to

From Les Temps modernes, *no. 318, January 1973.*

elect *their* government), were also denied permission to form groups and exercise popular or direct democracy. This would have been the only form of democracy appropriate to them, since they could not be separated from one another by their property.

Four years later, when the Convention replaced the land-owners' vote by universal suffrage, it still did not choose to repeal the Le Chapelier law. Consequently the workers, deprived once and for all of direct democracy, had to vote as landowners even though they owned nothing. Popular rallies, which took place often even though they were prohibited, became illegal even as they remained legitimate. What rose up in opposition to the assemblies elected by universal suffrage, first in 1794, then during the Second Republic in 1848, and lastly at the very beginning of the Third in 1870, were spontaneous though sometimes very large rallies of what could only be called the popular classes, or the people. In 1848 especially, it seemed that a worker's power, which had formed in the streets and in the National Workshops, was opposing the Chamber elected by universal suffrage, which had only recently been regained. The outcome is well known: in May and June of 1848, legality massacred legitimacy. Faced with the legitimate Paris Commune, the very legal Bordeaux Assembly, transferred to Versailles, had only to imitate this example.

At the end of the last century and the beginning of this one, things seemed to change. The right of the workers to strike was recognized, and the organization of trade unions was allowed. But the presidents of the Council, the heads of legality, would not tolerate the intermittent thrusts of popular power. Clemenceau in particular became known as a strikebreaker. All of them were obsessed by fear of the two powers. They refused to consider the coexistence of legitimate power, which had come into being here and there out of the real unity of the popular forces, with the falsely indivisible power which they exercised and which really depended on the infinitely wide dispersal of the voters. In fact, they had fallen into a contradiction which could only be resolved by civil war, since the function of civil war was to defuse this contradiction.

When we go to vote tomorrow, we will once again be substituting legal power for legitimate power. The first, which seems precise and perfectly clear-cut, has the effect of separating the voters in the name of universal suffrage. The second is still embryonic, diffuse, unclear even to itself. At this point it is indistinguishable from the vast libertarian and anti-hierarchical movement which one encounters everywhere but which is not at all organized yet. All the voters belong to very different groups. But to the ballot box they are not members of different groups but citizens. The polling booth standing in the lobby of a school or town hall is the symbol of all the acts of betrayal that the individual may commit against the group he belongs to. To each person it says: "No one can see you, you have only yourself to look to; you are going to be completely isolated when you make your decision, and afterwards you can hide that decision or lie about it." Nothing more is needed to transform all the voters who enter that hall into potential traitors to one another. Distrust increases the distance that separates them. If we want to fight against atomization, we must try to understand it first.

Men are not born in isolation: they are born into a family which *forms* them during their first years. Afterwards they will belong to different socioprofessional communities and will start a family themselves. They are atomized when large social forces—work conditions under the capitalist regime, private property, institutions, and so forth—bring pressure to bear upon the groups they belong to, breaking them up and reducing them to the units which supposedly compose them. The army, to mention only one example of an institution, does not look upon the recruit as an actual person; the recruit can only recognize himself by the fact that he belongs to existing groups. The army sees in him only the *man*, that is, the soldier—an abstract entity which is defined by the duties and the few rights which represent his relations with the military power. The soldier, which is just what the recruit is not but which military service is supposed to reduce him to, is in himself *other* than himself, and all the recruits in the same class are *identically* other. It is this very identity which separates them, since for each of them it represents only his predetermined general relationship with the army. During the hours of training, therefore, each is other than himself and at the same time identical with all the Others who are other than themselves. He can have real relations with his comrades only if they all cast off their identity as soldiers—say, at mealtimes or during the evening when they are in the barracks. Yet the word "atomization," so often used, does not convey the true situation of people who have been scattered and alienated by institutions. They cannot be reduced to the absolute solitude of the atom even though institutions try to replace their concrete relations with people by incidental connections. They cannot be excluded from all forms of social life: a soldier takes the bus, buys the newspaper, votes. All this presumes that he will make use of "collectives" along with the Others. But the collectives address him as a member of a series (the series of newspaper buyers, television watchers, etc.). He becomes in essence identical with all the other members, differing from them only by his serial number. We say that he has been serialized. One finds serialization in the practico-inert field, where matter mediates between men to the extent that men mediate between material objects. (For example, as soon as a man takes the steering wheel of his car he becomes no more than one driver among others and, because of this, helps reduce his own speed and everyone else's too, which is just the opposite of what he wanted, since he wanted to possess *his own* car.)

At that point, serial thinking is born in me, thinking

which is not my own thinking but that of the Other which I am and also that of all the Others. It must be called the thinking of powerlessness, because I produce it to the degree that I am Other, an enemy of myself and of the Others, and to the degree that I carry the Other everywhere with me. Let us take the case of a business where there has not been a strike for twenty or thirty years, but where the buying power of the worker is constantly falling because of the "high cost of living." Each worker begins to think about a protest movement. But twenty years of "social peace" have gradually established serial relations among the workers. Any strike—even if it were only for twenty-four hours—would require a regrouping of those people. At that point serial thinking—which separates them—vigorously resists the first signs of group thinking. Serial thinking will take several forms: it will be racist ("The immigrant workers would not go along with us"), sexist ("The women would not understand us"), hostile to other categories of society ("The small shopkeepers would not help us any more than the country people would"), distrustful ("The man near me is Other, so I don't know how he would react"), and so forth. All the separatist arguments represent not the thinking of the workers themselves but the thinking of the Others whom they have become and who want to keep their identity and their distance. If the regrouping should come about successfully, there will be no trace left of this pessimistic ideology. Its only function was to justify the maintenance of serial order and of an impotence that was in part tolerated and in part accepted.

Universal suffrage is an institution, and therefore a collective which atomizes or serializes individual men. It addresses the abstract entities within them—the citizens, who are defined by a set of political rights and duties, or in other words by their relation to the state and its institutions. The state makes citizens out of them by giving them, for example, the right to vote once every four years, on condition that they meet certain very general requirements—to be French, to be over twenty-one—which do not really characterize any of them.

From this point of view all citizens, whether they were born in Perpignan or in Lille, are perfectly identical, as we saw in the case of the soldiers. No interest is taken in the concrete problems that arise in their families or socioprofessional groups. Confronting them in their abstract solitude and their separation are the groups or parties soliciting their votes. They are told that they will be delegating their power to one or several of these political groups. But in order to "delegate its power," the series formed by the institution of the vote would itself have to possess at least a modicum of power. Now, these citizens, identical as they are and fabricated by the law, disarmed and separated by mistrust of one another, deceived but aware of their impotence, can never, as long as they remain serialized, form that sovereign group from which, we are told, all power emanates—the People. As we have seen, they have been granted universal suffrage for the purpose of atomizing them and keeping them from forming groups.

Only the parties, which were originally groups—though more or less bureaucratic and serialized—can be considered to have a modicum of power. In this case it would be necessary to reverse the classic formula, and when a party says "Choose me!" understand it to mean not that the voters would delegate their sovereignty to it, but that, refusing to unite in a group to obtain sovereignty, they would appoint one or several of the political communities already formed, in order to extend the power they have to the national limits. No party will be able to represent the series of citizens, because every party draws its power from itself, that is, from its communal structure. In any case, the series in its powerlessness cannot delegate any authority. Whereas the party, whichever one it might be, makes use of its authority to influence the series by demanding votes from it. The authority of the party over the serialized citizens is limited only by the authority of all the other parties put together.

When I vote, I abdicate my power—that is, the possibility everyone has of joining others to form a sovereign group, which would have no need of representatives. By voting I confirm the fact that we, the voters, are always other than ourselves and that none of us can ever desert the seriality in favor of the group, except through intermediaries. For the serialized citizen, to vote is undoubtedly to give his support to a party. But it is even more to vote for voting, as Kravetz says; that is, to vote for the political institution that keeps us in a state of powerless serialization.

We saw this in 1968 when de Gaulle asked the people of France, who had risen and formed groups, to vote—in other words, to lie down again and retreat into seriality. The non-institutional groups fell apart and the voters, identical and separate, voted for the U.D.R.* That party promised to defend them against the action of groups which they themselves had belonged to a few days earlier. We see it again today when Séguy asks for three months of social peace in order not to disturb the voters, but actually so that elections will be *possible*. For they no longer would be if fifteen million dedicated strikers, taught by the experience of 1968, refused to vote and went on to direct action. The voter must remain lying down, steeped in his own powerlessness. He will thus choose parties so that they can exert *their* authority and not his. Each man, locked in his right to vote just as the landowner is locked inside his land, will choose his masters for the next four years without seeing that this so-called right to vote is simply the refusal to allow him to unite with others in resolving the true problems by *praxis*.

The ballot method, always chosen by the groups in the Assembly and never by the voters, only aggravates things. Proportional representation did not save the voters from serial-

---

* Union pour la Défense de la République (the Gaullist party). [Translators' note.]

ity, but at least it used *all* the votes. The Assembly accurately
reflected political France, in other words repeated its serialized image, since the parties were represented proportionally,
by the number of votes each received. Our voting for a single
ticket, on the other hand, works on the opposite principle—
that, as one journalist rightly said, 49 percent equals zero.
If the U.D.R. candidates in a voting district obtain 50 percent of the votes in the second round, they are all elected.
The opposition's 49 percent is reduced to nothing: it corresponds to roughly half the population, which does not have
the right to be represented.

Take as an example a man who voted Communist in
1968 and whose candidates were not elected. Suppose he
votes for the Communist Party again in 1973. If the results
are different from the 1968 results, it will not be because of
him, since in both cases he voted for the same candidates.
For his vote to be meaningful, a certain number of voters
who voted for the present majority in 1968 would have to
grow tired of it, break away from it, and vote further to the
left. But it is not up to our man to persuade them; besides,
they are probably from a different milieu and he does not
even know them. Everything will take place elsewhere and
in a different way: through the propaganda of the parties,
through certain organs of the press. As for the Communist
Party voter, he has only to vote; this is all that is required
of him. He will vote, but he will not take part in the actions
that change the meaning of his vote. Besides, many of those
whose opinion can perhaps be changed may be against the
U.D.R. but are also deeply anti-Communist. They would
rather elect "reformers," who will thus become the arbiters
of the situation. It is not likely that the reformers will at this
point join the Socialist Party–Communist Party. They will
throw their weight in with the U.D.R. which, like them,
wants to maintain the capitalist regime. The U.D.R. and the
reformers become allies—and this is the objective meaning
of the Communist man's vote. His vote is in fact necessary

so that the Communist Party can keep its votes and even gain more votes. It is this gain which will reduce the number of majority candidates elected and will persuade them to throw themselves into the arms of the reformers. There is nothing to be said if we accept the rules of this fool's game.

But insofar as our voter is himself, in other words insofar as he is one specific man, he will not be at all satisfied with the result he has obtained as an identical Other. His class interests and his individual purposes have coincided to make him choose a leftist majority. He will have helped send to the Assembly a majority of the right and center in which the most important party will still be the U.D.R. When this man, therefore, puts his ballot in the box, the box will receive from the other ballots a different meaning from the one this voter wished to give it. Here again is serial action as it was seen in the practico-inert area.

We can go even further. Since by voting I affirm my institutionalized powerlessness, the established majority does not hesitate to cut, trim, and manipulate the electoral body in favor of the countryside and the cities that "vote the right way"—at the expense of the suburbs and outlying districts that "vote the wrong way." Even the seriality of the electorate is thereby changed. If it were perfect, one vote would be equal to any other. But in reality, 120,000 votes are needed to elect a Communist deputy, while only 30,000 can send a U.D.R. candidate to the Assembly. One majority voter is worth four Communist Party voters. The point is that the majority voter is casting his ballot against what we would have to call a supermajority, meaning a majority which intends to remain in place by other means than the simple seriality of votes.

Why am I going to vote? Because I have been persuaded that the only political act in my life consists of depositing my ballot in the box once every four years? But that is the very opposite of an act. I am only revealing my powerlessness and obeying the power of a party. Furthermore, the value of my vote varies according to whether I obey one party or another. For this reason the majority of the future Assembly will be based solely on a coalition, and the decisions it makes will be compromises which will in no way reflect the desires expressed by my vote. In 1959 a majority voted for Guy Mollet because he claimed he could make peace in Algeria sooner than anyone else. The Socialist government which came to power decided to intensify the war, and this induced many voters to leave the series—which never knows for whom or for what it is voting—and join clandestine action groups. This was what they should have done much earlier, but in fact the unlikely result of their votes was what exposed the powerlessness of universal suffrage.

Actually, everything is quite clear if one thinks it over and reaches the conclusion that indirect democracy is a hoax. Ostensibly, the elected Assembly is the one which reflects public opinion most faithfully. But there is only one sort of public opinion, and it is serial. The imbecility of the mass media, the government pronouncements, the biased or incomplete reporting in the newspapers—all this comes to seek us out in our serial solitude and load us down with wooden ideas, formed out of what we think others will think. Deep within us there are undoubtedly demands and protests, but because they are not echoed by others, they wither away and leave us with a "bruised spirit" and a feeling of frustration. So when we are called to vote, I, the Other, have my head stuffed with petrified ideas which the press or television has piled up there. They are serial ideas which are expressed through my vote, but they are not *my* ideas. The institutions of bourgeois democracy have split me apart: there is me and there are all the Others they tell me I am (a Frenchman, a soldier, a worker, a taxpayer, a citizen, and so on). This splitting-up forces us to live with what psychiatrists call a perpetual identity crisis. Who am I, in the end? An Other identical with all the others, inhabited by these impotent thoughts which come into being everywhere and are not actually *thought* anywhere? Or am I myself? And who is voting? I do not recognize myself any more.

There are some people who will vote, they say, "just to change the old scoundrels for new ones," which means that as they see it the otherthrow of the U.D.R. majority has absolute priority. And I can understand that it would be nice to throw out these shady politicians. But has anyone thought about the fact that in order to overthrow them, one is forced to replace them with another majority which will keep the same electoral principles?

The U.D.R., the reformers, and the Communist Party–Socialist Party are in competition. These parties stand on a common ground which consists of indirect representation, their hierarchic power, and the powerlessness of the citizens, in other words, the "bourgeois system." Yet it should give us pause that the Communist Party, which claims to be revolutionary, has, since the beginning of peaceful coexistence, been reduced to seeking power in the bourgeois manner by accepting the institution of bourgeois suffrage. It is a matter of who can put it over on the citizens best. The U.D.R. talks about order and social peace, and the Communist Party tries to make people forget its revolutionary image. At present the Communists are succeeding so well in this, with the eager help of the Socialists, that if they were to take power because of our votes, they would postpone the revolution indefinitely and would become the most stable of the electoral parties. Is there so much advantage in changing? In any case, the revolution will be drowned in the ballot boxes—which is not surprising, since they were made for that purpose.

Yet some people try to be Machiavellian, in other words, try to use their votes to obtain a result that is not serial. They aim to send a Communist Party–Socialist Party majority to the Assembly in hopes of forcing Pompidou to end the pretense—that is, to dissolve the Chamber, force us into active battle, class against class or rather group against group, perhaps into civil war. What a strange idea—to serialize us, in keeping with the enemy's wishes, so that he will react with violence and force us to group together. And it is a mistaken idea. In order to be a Machiavel, one must deal with certainties whose effect is predictable. Such is not the case here: one cannot predict with certainty the consequences of serialized suffrage. What can be foreseen is that the U.D.R. will lose seats and the Communist Party–Socialist Party and the reformers will gain seats. Nothing else is likely enough for us to base a strategy on it. There is only one sign: a survey made by the I.F.O.P. and published in *France-Soir* on December 4, 1972, showed 45 percent for the Communist Party–Socialist Party, 40 percent for the U.D.R., and 15 percent for the reformers. It also revealed a curious fact: there are many more votes for the Communist Party–Socialist Party than there are people convinced that this coalition will win. Therefore—and always allowing for the fallibility of surveys—many people seem to favor voting for the left, yet apparently feel certain that it will not receive the majority of the votes. And there are even more people for whom the elimination of the U.D.R. is the most important thing but who are not particularly eager to replace it by the left.

So as I write these comments on January 5, 1973, I find a U.D.R.–reformer majority likely. If this is the case, Pompidou will not dissolve the Assembly; he will prefer to make do with the reformers. The majority party will become somewhat supple, there will be fewer scandals—that is, the government will arrange it so that they are harder to discover—and Jean-Jacques Servan-Schreiber and Lecannet will enter the government. That is all. Machiavellianism will therefore turn against the small Machiavels.

If they want to return to direct democracy, the democracy of people fighting against the system, of individual men fighting against the seriality which transforms them into things, why not start here? To vote or not to vote is all the same. To abstain is in effect to confirm the new majority, whatever it may be. Whatever we may do about it, we will have done nothing if we do not fight at the same time—and that means starting today—against the system of indirect democracy which deliberately reduces us to powerlessness. We must try, each according to his own resources, to organize the vast anti-hierarchic movement which fights institutions everywhere.

Index

Jean-Paul Sartre was born in Paris in 1905. Educated at the École normale, he then taught philosophy in provincial *lycées*, and in 1938 published his first novel, *Nausea*. During the war, he participated in the Resistance and completed the major work which eventually established his reputation as an existential philosopher—*Being and Nothingness* (1943). After the Liberation, he founded the socialist journal *Les Temps Modernes*. He has been a prolific playwright, producing among other works, *No Exit* (1947), *The Devil and the Good Lord* (1951), and *The Condemned of Altona* (1959). In 1960, he published his second basic philosophical work, *Critique of Dialectical Reason*. In 1964, his account of his childhood, *The Words*, received world-wide acclaim. That same year he was awarded the Nobel Prize for Literature, which he refused. In 1971–1972, the first three volumes of his ambitious study of Flaubert's life and work appeared. *Between Existentialism and Marxism* (1974) and *Sartre on Theater* (1976) have been previously published by Pantheon.